Own The Life You Deserve

NO ONE ELSE WILL

Paul R. Goudreault

Big Water Press
Lake of the Ozarks, Missouri

Copyright © 2025 by Paul R. Goudreault.

All rights reserved. No part of this publication may be reproduced, distributed or transmitted in any form or by any means, including photocopying, recording, or other electronic or mechanical methods, without the prior written permission of the publisher, except in the case of brief quotations embodied in critical reviews and certain other noncommercial uses permitted by copyright law. For permission requests, write to the publisher, addressed "Attention: Permissions Coordinator," at the address below.

Paul R. Goudreault /Big Water Press
Camdenton, MO 65020
www.bigwaterpress.com

Book Layout ©2017 BookDesignTemplates.com
Cover Design by Wise Bear Creative www.wisebearcreative.com

Ordering Information:
Quantity sales. Special discounts are available on quantity purchases by corporations, associations, and others. For details, contact Big Water Press at Contact@bigwaterpress.com.

Own The Life You Deserve/ Paul R. Goudreault. —1st ed.
ISBN 978-1-7364200-2-7 Hardcover
ISBN 978-1-7364200-3-4 Paperback

Recommendations

Tim Ranf, Pioneer Technical Services, CEO –
"Paul has been an invaluable advisor to me personally and to my company for years now. With this book, he provides the insight and guidance needed to create better and stronger connections that will support the growth of employees and their employers. If you want to lead to a more fulfilling career and life (and all of us do), Paul's process will help you get there."

Scott Chafin, ENTACT – Chief Commercial Officer –
"Paul has drawn upon his experience to craft a warm, thoughtful, and practical approach to personal career assessment and improvement."

Rosa Santillan, Opti, Project Manager –
"Own The Life You Deserve" offers invaluable tools and insights for cultivating a harmonious work-life partnership. This book also encourages self-reflection across all stages of the ADAPT Career Lifecycle Model while bridging generational biases. Paul's conversational, chapter-by-chapter approach feels like a thoughtful discussion with a trusted friend, guiding readers towards a more fulfilling life and career.

Jim Holland, Pinnacle Engineering, CEO –

"Building a strong employee culture is important to us and our firm. Paul's book brings forward so many good ideas and tools to help us continue to engage and retain our employees. I highly recommend this book!"

Jeff Dutton, Eurofins, Sales Director--

"As an older Millennial with three children, a small homestead, side businesses, and a full-time job that requires a fair amount of travel, balance is the aspect of life that I find to be the most elusive. This book - full of wisdom clearly earned via experience and insightful anecdotes - helped me to take a serious look in the mirror, assess my situation, and begin to prioritize my life in a manner that has led to reduced stress, greater effectiveness at the office and at home, and heightened confidence about where to focus my attention for life's journey ahead."

Bob Karls, Antea USA, Inc., senior consultant, president –

"My nieces and nephews in college have Paul's first book "Own Your Career-No One Else Will". They have told me that 'no one else has really engaged with me on these topics, it really gave me something to think about – thanks!'. I am glad to see Paul's next book is available. Paul has tackled many of the topics that are either never discussed directly or are touching on tough topics like generational differences in a clear and open manner. I have a great gift idea for all my family!"

Contents

INTRODUCTION I

CHAPTER 1 - WHAT CAN I EXPECT? 1

    WHY: TO SHARE & ENCOURAGE 2

    WHAT: THE CAREER-LIFE PARTNERING MODEL 4

    WHO: TO A CAREER AND LIFE WELL LIVED 7

    SUMMARY 10

CHAPTER 2 - FINDING COMMON GROUND 13

    BABY BOOMERS 17

    GENERATION X 19

    MILLENNIALS 22

    GENERATION Z 25

    GENERATION ALPHA 27

    SUMMARY 28

CHAPTER 3 - GENERATIONAL BIAS 31

    CROSS-GENERATIONAL FRAMEWORK 33

        CONTROL VS. FLEXIBILITY 34

COMMITMENT TO COMPANY VS. COMMITMENT TO SELF 36

SHARE VALUE VS. SOCIAL VALUE 37

DIGIT VS. DIGITAL 39

PATIENCE VS. IMPATIENCE 41

AUTHORITY VS. EMPATHY 43

SUMMARY 45

CHAPTER 4 - A CAREER SHOULDN'T BE A MYSTERY 49

CAREER ASPIRATIONS 50

THE ADAPT CAREER LIFECYCLE MODEL 54

ACQUIRE 55

DEVELOP 57

APPLY 59

PRODUCE 61

TRANSITION 63

SUMMARY 65

CHAPTER 5 - CAREER-LIFE PARTNERING MODEL 69

WHY PARTNERING? 69

CAREER ISN'T A BAD WORD 71

INTRODUCING THE CAREER-LIFE PARTNERING MODEL........72

SUMMARY..80

CHAPTER 6 - CAREER-LIFE CARE ASSESSMENT........................83

CAREER CARE 85

10 CAREER BUILDING BLOCKS......................................86

LIFE CARE 90

10 LIFE BUILDING BLOCKS 91

OPPORTUNITIES & CHALLENGES......................................94

SUMMARY..100

CHAPTER 7 - CAREER-LIFE PARTNERING MATRIX 103

INFORMED, ENLIGHTENED, & PURPOSEFUL 104

INTRODUCING THE CAREER-LIFE PARTNERING MATRIX.....106

SUMMARY..111

CHAPTER 8 - ESSENTIAL PARTNERING ELEMENTS 113

PARTNERING AIN'T EASY 113

ORGANIZATIONAL CULTURE 116

COMMUNICATION 117

COMPROMISING 118

POWER..120

DISAPPOINTMENT 121

MAKING CHOICES	123
INVESTMENT NEEDS	124
BOUNDARIES	125
SUMMARY	127
CHAPTER 9 - CAREER LIFE PARTNERING PLAN	**131**
LET'S PUT IT ALL TOGETHER!	134
STEP 1. ASPIRATIONS	135
STEP 2. ADAPT LIFECYCLE	135
STEP 3. CAREER AND LIFE BUILDING BLOCKS	136
STEP 4. THREE- AND FIVE-YEAR CAREER GOALS	137
STEP 5. THREE- AND FIVE-YEAR LIFE GOALS	138
STEP 6. CAREER AND LIFE GAPS	138
STEP 7. CAREER-LIFE ROADMAP	139
SUMMARY	140
CHAPTER 10 - CONTINUING YOUR CAREER-LIFE JOURNEY	**143**
UNDERSTANDING WORKFORCE EXPECTATIONS	144
CREATING A CAREER-LIFE VISION (ASPIRATION)	144
OWNING YOUR CAREER-LIFE PATH	145
REFLECTING ON YOUR PROGRESS	145

A LIFELONG JOURNEY OF CAREER-LIFE PARTNERING 145

PLANNING YOUR JOURNEY 146

SUMMARY 147

AFTERWORD 149

ACKNOWLEDGEMENTS 151

APPENDIX I 153

APPENDIX II 167

APPENDIX III 173

To my family: Katie, my wife and life partner for over 50 years; my daughter Monet; and my son Adrien. It is not easy to develop a career and life that is meaningful and purposeful. They always understood the challenges and were my best friends and advocates. Thanks for putting up with me!

To all career developers: Whatever career or life path you choose, please leave a lasting positive effect on those you care for most. I know you will!

"It's not the years in your life that count. It's the life in your years." —Abraham Lincoln

Introduction

"Life gets mighty precious when there's less of it to waste." – Bonnie Raitt

Sacrificing your life for your career is not acceptable.

Maybe you feel stuck in a job, or you are "burned out." Are you spending enough time enjoying your life, or are you "too busy working"? Do you have enough time to pursue your passions, enjoy your friends, or take care of your health? Today it is more challenging than ever to navigate a successful career and a meaningful life together, where each is complementing and supporting the other. The distractions of today's world can be overwhelming and pull your focus from what truly matters to you. This is a good time to refresh what you have learned about developing a career and living your best life.

We're not talking about "work-life balance" here. While it may be an easy term to use, it really doesn't describe the challenges and opportunities of building a purposeful career and life. Let me help you develop a mindset where you can look at your career as a partner, not a foe; as a friend, not an enemy. This may be your opportunity to challenge your career and also partner with it to build the life you deserve.

I would like to share with you my career and life experiences and those of my colleagues and my mentees. There are many things we don't learn intentionally, and one of these things is how to be successful in both our careers and our lives! This book is focused on providing you the tools capable of supporting your career-life journey. Whether you are an employee guiding your career and life or a manager responsible for developing your employees, I encourage you to utilize the concepts and tools provided to you in this book. Provided are several essential ideas that will help you create the career-life balance you desire:

- ✅ ***Cross Generational Framework:*** *Helps us understand the generational differences we inherit when envisioning our career and life*

- ✅ ***ADAPT Career Lifecycle Model****: A five-stage career lifecycle to help you understand where you might be in your career journey*

- ✅ ***Career-Life Care Assessment:*** *You will immediately recognize from your self-assessment which of the 20 Career and Life Building Blocks are important to you today*

- ✅ ***Career-Life Partnering Matrix:*** *Quickly identify your current career life relationship and learn how to move your career and life forward*

- ✅ ***Essential Partnering Elements:*** *Assess your company or organization as a reliable partner*

- ✅ ***Career-Life Partnering Plan:*** *Create a custom action plan for future career and life growth*

My previous book, ***Own Your Career – No One Else Will,*** began as a helpful guide to my 20-something kids and grew in scope to support all career developers. ***Own The Life You Deserve – No One Else Will*** is a result of my work with professional career developers looking to grow their careers and companies seeking ways to retain their employees. Developing a sustainable and meaningful career and a life to be proud of is not easy. You deserve a career and life that will allow you to explore new cultures, challenge the way you think about life and gives you the financial freedom to reinvest in yourself. If you are an employer, building an inquisitive and engaged workforce will lead to stability in your human capacity.

Taking your career development and your life plan into your own hands in this deliberate way can be intimidating—but also very rewarding. You can develop a career that aligns with your passions, your life plan, and builds personal wealth. Are you ready for a lifelong career journey? Are you ready for life's many challenges and opportunities? Regardless of your age, you will be successful by taking ownership of your career and life, remaining focused on your career aspiration and what is important to you in your life.

This book is not an academic study. Rather, it's a practical guide for career and life planning. I hope the book will be easy to use and informative. I am confident that you will reach your career and life aspirations.

Lastly, I have developed an on-line application for you to assess your career-life partnership. You can complete the career-life care assessment and receive your very own, individualize report. Please feel free to access the application at www.PaulGoudreault.com. Use Promo Code: Book.

You deserve both a career and a life well lived!

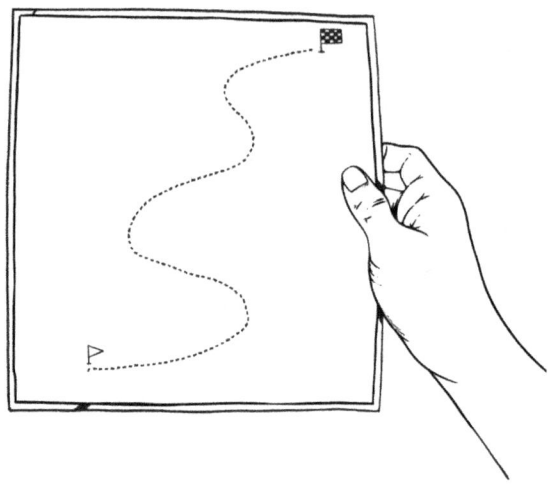

CHAPTER 1

What Can I Expect?

**"The unexamined life is not worth living."
— Socrates**

The purpose of this book is to support you in developing a career that allows you to achieve your life goals! Creating the right relationship with your career is not easy. Today's career journeys are much more complicated than they have been in the past. While there are many new opportunities in developing a career, there are also many challenges. Seldom do today's careers follow a straight line from point A to point B; rather, careers develop through exploration. You will have several jobs working for a company, for an organization, or for yourself. To complicate matters, the employee-employer expectations are constantly changing. You have a long and challenging journey ahead of you. Consider this short list of questions being asked in the workplace today:

- *Can I continue to work remotely?*
- *Are my employer-provided benefits sufficient for my future?*

> ◎ *Will my industry or job be marginalized by AI?*
>
> ◎ *Will there be another layoff?*
>
> ◎ *Can I continue to remain self-employed with my current skills?*

Fending for yourself seems to be the normal path to success. Your relationship with your employer can be complicated. Many times, your goals will be misaligned, expectations will be unrealistic, or opportunities to secure a fulfilling career and life will be unclear. But I believe that you can create a career-life partnering mindset that will help you to navigate a career and life journey that will be challenging, exciting, and rewarding.

Your career-life journey is uniquely yours and no one else's!

Why: To Share & Encourage

Motivation is gained by the successes you see.

Why did I write this book? My passion today is to support employees and companies in creating the right behaviors so that employers can rely on sustainable resources and employees can build the career and a life they envision. I routinely coach and mentor young career developers and company leaders. What I have learned from them is that mapping your career is only half the battle. Achieving your life goals while having a meaningful career is the real challenge. I have become obsessed with creating a simple Career-Life Partnering Model that everyone can use in the way that works for them. This book is designed to help you visualize your career and your life, provide guideposts along the way, and support you in developing the next chapter in your career-life book. The goal is to provide an easy-to-read supplement to other information you gather about career development and life choices. You can expect the ideas that I present here have been lived and experienced by me, many of my colleagues, and my mentees.

Don't wait till the end of your career to assess your life.

My wife, Katie, and I make it a priority to travel together. Recently, we were on a river cruise on the Rhine and the Danube. Wonderful trip, but I was surprised how people talked about their careers. An attorney from Chicago said, "I hated every minute of my career; I was a hostage to my firm." A mail carrier from Minneapolis, who retired after 45 years in the United States Postal Service, told us, "I miss my job. I miss the people on my route; I got to know them and their families. I miss them all!" Obviously, there are many reasons why people either enjoy or dislike their careers. Sometimes it is the profession, their employer, or their colleagues. Generally, we can relate disappointments in our careers to the lack of attention paid to what is important and/or how our careers affect our lives!

Today, connectivity is everything. It is impossible to disconnect! While wonderful in some ways, there are also serious challenges. Technology, connectivity, and the global nature of business have created a workplace that demands more and more. This is not going away. These changes and the responses by business and society will only accelerate.

Are you willing to:

- Set boundaries around your work?
- Work efficiently to minimize your time at work?
- Proactively spend time with family and friends?
- Invest in your well-being?
- Pursue your passion?
- Build financial freedom?

Your career, your life and your demands will continue to change. However, one thing that should not change, is your desire to challenge your career and life journey to create a path unique to you!

Partner with your career to achieve your life goals.

What: The Career-Life Partnering Model

Your career aspirations should be aligned with your life goals.

For all of us, complexity increases with time. One of my new goals in life, is to keep things simple. Sometimes complexity helps, it can create innovative ideas, wonderful visions and longer-term inspiration. Taking complexity and simplifying it is an art. Yes, simplifying can limit your perspective or drive to premature solutions, but it can also help address our greatest challenges and opportunities. The Career Life Partnering Model is a framework and a set of tools that anyone can use to evaluate, prioritize and focus on those career and life challenges or opportunities to build a meaningful career and life. I routinely use the Career Life Partnering Model in my mentoring. I recently coached a cohort from an engineering & consulting firm. This is what I heard after use of the Career Life Partnering Model:

> *"I like my coworkers and clients, but I need to invest more in friendships and family."*
>
> *"I have a great advisory team and mentors, but I sometimes lack the confidence to lead teams."*
>
> *"I want my career to inspire my personal life and provide me with financial flexibility."*
>
> *"My top three areas of improvement include investing in myself, spending more time with my family, and creating a network of professional relationships."*
>
> *"I provide my time, my energy, and my knowledge to my career. I get paid fairly, and I get a sense of accomplishment and lasting relationships from my career."*

The core of the Career-Life Partnering Model includes a Career-Life Care Assessment composed of twenty essential Career and Life Building Blocks, where ten building blocks address your career progress and ten apply to your life goals. It is up to you to determine your progress on each and your top challenges and opportunities.

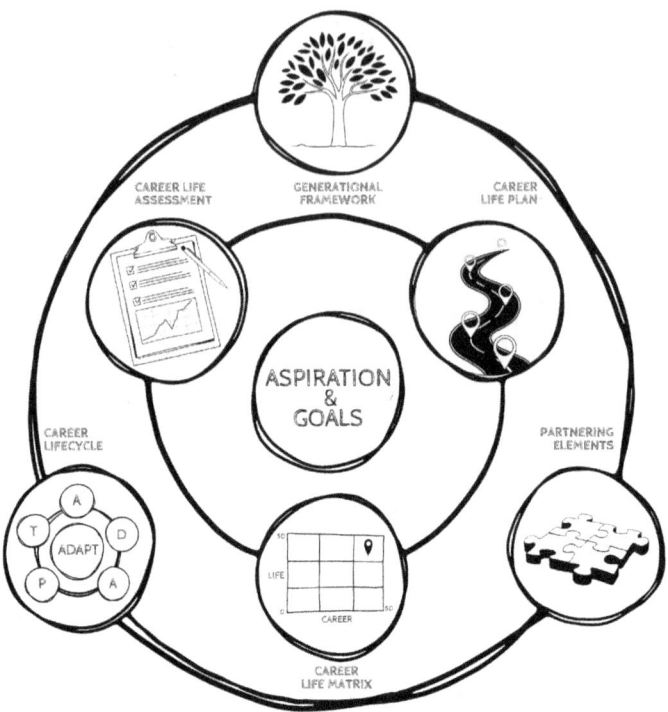

In addition to the Career-Life Care Assessment, also included in this book are a Career-Life Partnering Matrix and a Career-Life Partnering Plan. The Career-Life Partnering Matrix will allow you to quickly visualize your career and life priorities and help you move your career-life partnership in the right direction. The Career-Life Partnering Plan will look at where your priorities are today and assist you in plotting your course over the next three to five years. The Career-Life Partnering Plan can help you by identifying future roles, any gaps you need to fill, and what your life goals may be over time.

The Career-Life Partnering Model will help you quickly assess how effective you are in partnering with your career for a life you deserve.

Does your career support your life goals?

Who: To a Career and Life Well Lived

Employers and employees exchange value, not work!

In my mentoring practice, I am actively supporting employers and employees by helping them achieve mutual success in the workforce. This requires the development of meaningful careers that offer a fulfilling life to the employee. As we will discuss, the old paradigms of company commitment, stability, and a secure future have given way to the new realities of work, business, and life. Employers and employees have found themselves in a position of exchanging value: Employees give themselves to work, and the employer gives themself to the employee. The balance of this exchange has been typically driven by the employer, but this is changing. Employers are learning that employees are most effective at work if they value what they are doing.

In researching this book, I have worked hard to get a cross-generational perspective via interviews with several of my colleagues and mentees. Many of my colleagues are either Baby Boomers or Gen Xers, while my mentees are generally Millennials or Gen Zers. I asked them each five questions and to share advice they would like to give to fellow career developers.

The five questions are:

- ✓ *How do you define a career?*
- ✓ *What are the challenges of building a career?*
- ✓ *How do you define a successful life?*

> ✔ *How do you balance a career and life?*
>
> ✔ *What are your expectations for your career?*

While the responses to these questions vary, they tend to reflect the generational differences in my colleagues and mentees. My biggest takeaway from these discussions was that everyone has a unique perspective on their career, and everyone is working hard to balance their career with their life. Also, to my surprise, few of my colleagues or mentees have taken any concrete steps in evaluating their career and life positions, priorities, or next steps.

I will be integrating my interview responses into the following chapters, but as a summary, this is what I heard:

> *"A career allows me to leverage my skills and passion to generate the opportunities to live the life I want."*
>
> *"My career is more than a job, I want a career to support my lifestyle?"*
>
> *"My challenges are finding a company culture fit, growth opportunities, and a location compatible with my family."*
>
> *"I need to remain focused, patient, motivated, and remove any self-doubts."*
>
> *"Keeping engaged in my career is difficult. I have not yet found something that excites me."*
>
> *"I want to meaningfully impact others in a positive manner."*
>
> *"Family first, career second."*
>
> *"I look for fulfillment, at work and in life."*

"Cast a vision, find mentors, and remain flexible."

I am hopeful that you, as the reader, will be interested in more of these insights and be motivated to dig into the Career-Life Partnering Model. This book has been designed with all career and life developer ages in mind. Let's see how these insights can help you!

Are you evaluating your career and life positions, priorities, and next steps?

Summary

This book and the Career-Life Partnering Model are structured so you can use the concepts and tools to inspect and prioritize your career and life path. There is work to do. I hope you will find value and will pursue those challenges and opportunities you identify, helping you come closer to your career and life goals. As said by many others, we are all on a journey, but its sometimes nice to check in on our progress and ask the questions to help us reach our goals. Let's explore how you:

- ✓ *Define your relationship with your career.*
- ✓ *Spend enough time on what matters at work and in your life.*
- ✓ *Define the value you get from your career.*
- ✓ *Leverage your opportunities and take on your challenges.*
- ✓ *Partner with your career to achieve your life goals.*

Remember, you are in the driver's seat. It is up to you to set your destination, map your course, and start your journey. You can create your own unique path forward, challenge yourself, and reach both your desire career and life outcomes.

To a happy and fulfilling journey!

CHAPTER 2

Finding Common Ground

"The noblest pleasure is the joy of understanding." – Leonardo da Vinci

Companies and managers, please take the time to understand your employees.

Partnering with your career is only possible if your company encourages it, your managers support it, and you are willing to take ownership of your career and life. Great companies are in tune with their employees and understand the benefits of creating a compelling vision, a purposeful mission, and an environment where the behaviors of their leaders are consistent with the values of the company. In many industries, the highest rates of voluntary turnover are employees who have been with the company from one to three years. Why is that? I think it is because the company, the managers, and the employee are not aligned and do not understand their mutual needs.

Developing a partnering relationship starts with finding common understanding. Companies, managers, and employees should inspect how they deliver value to each other. If you are an employee, what are your career aspirations and where are you in your career lifecycle? Certainly, everyone's view on their career and life is unique. Furthermore, it should be obvious that not everyone you work with will be the same stage in their career lifecycle.

If you are a manager, you are being pulled in different directions. Priorities can be overwhelming. It is not easy being a manager and meeting the needs of your organization and your team members. The effort is high, and it takes a commitment to make the time to guide, coach, and inspire your employees. However, if you do recognize each employee's unique needs, you will have a more effective and durable team to help you with your accountabilities.

Managers are likely leading and supporting cross-generational teams. Your individual employees' perspectives on work, career, and life may differ from yours. Your primary assignment as a manager is to use the resources you have to create the greatest value to your firm, company, or organization. Much like a jigsaw puzzle, each piece is different and fits with the others to form the desired picture.

As a manager, have you ever thought:

> ◎ *I wish Amenda would realize how important her assignments are to the company.*
>
> ◎ *Why doesn't Albert want to take on more responsibility?*
>
> ◎ *If I only had more Alex's on my team!*

- *Why does everyone want a raise and a promotion every year?*

- *If we all worked a little harder, we could be more successful.*

Helping individuals on your team achieve both their career and their life goals can be one of the most satisfying aspects of a manager's role. While I hope I have been able to support my teams, I have also missed way too many opportunities to help my teams achieve their career and life goals. I regret one specific opportunity many years ago when one of my team members was always running out of money, before pay day. He approached me and asked if I could lend him some money, my response: "Jack, I can help you out here at work, but I can't help you outside of work". My view was that he was fairly paid, had work hour flexibility and was a well-liked team member. What I did not realize, he was an addict and needed help for his addiction. I could have and should have done more! Addiction took Jack's life a few years later at a young age.

My lesson, you really do not know your teams struggles or needs unless you purposely care and engage with them as a partner. Key to a true partnership between manager and employee is a shared understanding of generational biases and differences in the workplace and the importance of both career development and life goal attainment.

Everyone is unique.

My observations on generational bias are seen through my interactions with organizations, mentees, and colleagues. Partnering with a career requires you to understand your colleagues, be willing to adapt, and have a little fun by celebrating differences.

The workforce will continue to change. Although the Baby Boomers are working later, Generation X and Millennials well surpass the number of Baby Boomers. The leadership within organizations is transitioning to Generation X.

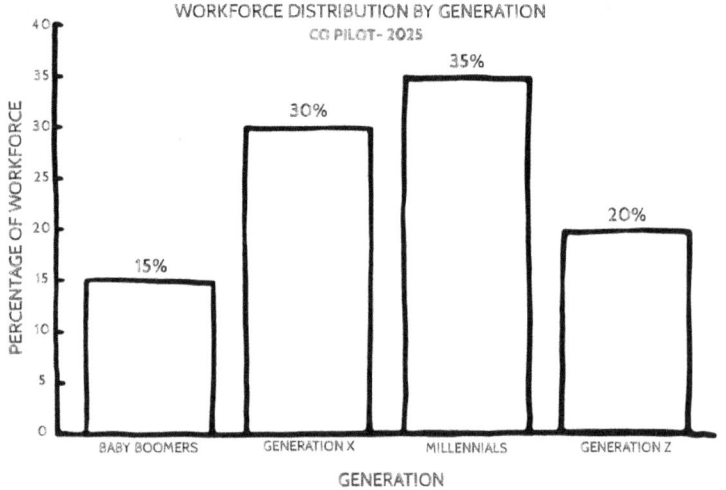

Baby Boomers

Work hard, keep your head down, and you will get what you deserve.

Baby Boomers are typically defined as being born between 1946–1964. How can you recognize a Baby Boomer? Most Baby Boomers in the workplace are planning their retirement or are passively retired "in place." Being a Baby Boomer myself, I don't mean to cast a negative light on those who have worked hard for more than forty years and have contributed in numerous ways to their professions and their families and friends. At the same time, Boomers tend to talk about how things were; they admire hard work and commitment. Most Boomers are likely financially capable of managing a retirement but stay in the workforce for the personal challenge, the long-term benefits, or their egos. The Boomers, in many cases, are the last of the "defined benefit pension" generation. These pension plans accumulate lifetime benefits with increased years of service, so why not continue to grow your retirement accounts until the magical next buyout?!

Companies have a dilemma managing their aging workforce. Organizations need to continuously balance institutional knowledge with increasing costs. An age pyramid drives many organizations, realizing only so many "top-end" positions can be maintained. In many businesses, it is expected to have and annual 15-20% employee turnover (voluntary and involuntary). Boomers who remain at work will have leadership, management, or client account management roles. In addition, a few key technical experts will remain to coach and mentor junior staff.

Outside of work, Boomers are realizing how hard they have worked for so long. They have a newfound need to spend more time with family and friends and taking care of themselves. Personal time becomes more valuable and the desire for it often alters professional ambitions. The need to separate career and life becomes more obvious for the aging Boomer.

Their expectations for the workplace differ significantly from younger generations. Baby Boomers tend to make work their identity. They are concerned about ageism in the workplace, and they have a strong desire to mentor younger generations. They value:

- *A strong work ethic*
- *Company loyalty*
- *Face-to-face communication*
- *Face-to-face work (skeptical of remote work)*
- *Job stability and benefits*
- *Organizational hierarchy*

Baby Boomers provide the company with a stable base of institutional knowledge. They can help promote the desired culture of the organization and support the development of new leaders. You may already or will be reporting to a Baby Boomer, so understanding their "employer-employee relationship model" is key.

Working with a Baby Boomer can be a real joy, or it can become frustrating. Boomers tend to be more patient and understand the culture and speed of the organization. Most organizations move slowly, and one of a Boomer's strengths is pacing change against the organizational appetite for change. In some cases, however, Boomers purposely limit innovation and change to assure their personal value to the firm. Hence the joy and the frustration!

> **Planning retirement or retiring in place.**

Generation X

> **Organizations depend on Gen X to drive results.**

Generation Xers are typically identified as those born between 1965–1980. Gen Xers often bridge the gap between Baby Boomers and Millennials. This generation has seen significant advancements in technology, economic turmoil, and instability in the workplace throughout their careers. Many Gen Xers have a mix of traditional values and the adaptation to new ways of working. Their adaptability and pragmatic outlook make them valuable assets in the evolving workplace.

Gen Xers in the workplace are generally in the "Produce" career lifecycle stage (Chapter 4). They will be in positions of power and influence, on leadership teams, or taking on key company imperatives. Simply stated, they are optimizing their positions within their organizations and likely looking out for "numero uno." Gen Xers are faced with significant demands from their organizations and are driven to achieve their goals. Many Gen Xers have more advancement opportunities ahead of them, but they are becoming more and more limited. They are competing to get to or remain on top of the hill.

This generation is however "corporate leery." They have seen the removal of defined benefit pension plans, increasing numbers of layoffs, and a host of mergers and acquisitions. Managing organizational power, making a competitive wage (and bonus), and optimizing professional opportunities are significant priorities for this generation. Gen Xers have their retirement age and money number but haven't reached it yet. If they are performing, they are well compensated and see no need to move on to retirement or a new opportunity. At the same time, Gen Xers are most vulnerable to leadership changes and need to be nimble to keep up with the future direction of the organization.

Gen Xers tend to be integrators, meaning they mix work and life, remaining connected and engaged in both pursuits simultaneously. Emails and text messages after hours and during weekend are common with this group. Responsiveness to priorities shows commitment and is valued highly. Organizations depend on Gen Xers to drive organizational results. If you are part of a winning team, your value will become clear and worth the effort.

Here's some of what Gen Xers may view as important at work:

- *Power and influence*
- *Independence and autonomy*
- *Adaptability*
- *Loyalty (to a point)*
- *Entrepreneurial spirit*
- *Goals and incentives*

- *Professional advancement*
- *Equity and value*
- *Desire to coach*

Gen Xers are great connectors between Baby Boomers and Millennials. While they share many of the Baby Boomer's values, they also recognize that the workplace has changed and know how to navigate that change.

If you are not a Gen Xer, you are likely working for one! If you have been in the organization for a while, you have demonstrated your individual performance. For the Gen Xer, a primary objective is to drive greater results via an effective team. An effective team that achieves his or her goals and is recognized by the organization for its success is a reflection of their value to the organization. Working with a Gen Xer is demanding, is fast paced, and requires discipline. Communication is important. Gen Xers don't like surprises that might be challenged by their peers or organizational leaders. Be comfortable working with defined goals, routine tracking and monitoring, and a continued sense of "let's do better."

Corporate leery, but good Baby Boomer and Millennial connectors.

Millennials

There is more to life than work.

Millennials, born between 1981–1996, have views on work that have been influenced by technological advancement and sociocultural changes. Their approach to their careers reflects the first significant change in values and priorities compared to previous generations. The Millennials are the first to seek work-life balance by beginning to prioritize life outside of work over the work grind. In addition, this generation is the first to recognize the value of organizations beyond their business or service. They have put on notice organizations, brands, and businesses that they expect them to provide positive social contributions to our communities.

If Boomers are managing the business and Gen Xers are driving the results, Millennials are doing the work! The Millennial workforce is the largest of all generational workforces. The Millennials in your organization are focused on generating results efficiently—with the least amount of effort—while leveraging technology. They are NOT lazy, just more efficient than older generations. Resist telling a Millennial how to do something; just tell them what needs to be done and why.

One of the biggest difficulties for Millennials in the workforce is to remain challenged by their jobs. They are generally independent, not afraid of change, and always looking for opportunities to grow. Millennials are financially insecure (many are starting their financial literacy and have many new expenses), and they are easily persuaded to pursue opportunities to seek meaningful work and better income. Millennials will look for new opportunities that offer a strong cultural or work type fit. More than any prior generation, Millennials are not afraid to change industries or organizations or to refocus their career.

Millennials place a priority on their time away from work. My Millennial mentees work hard to organize and complete work so they can take time away from work. Part of executing work efficiently is organizing team assignments and work delivery milestones to make it as easy as possible to complete the work. Leveraging technology to minimize work and rework is a priority. Finding time to care for a pet, raise a child, stay in touch with friends, or travel for new experiences are important for this generation. Their career must support their life desires and keep them challenged in meaningful work, or the Millennial will seek other opportunities.

Lastly, but not least notable, Millennials are the first generation to dive into the gig economy. Don't be surprised if your Millennial employee has another job (or more) independent and separate from your organization.

Here's how Millennials may view work:

- *Work-life balance*
- *Purpose and impact*
- *Career growth and development*
- *Opportunities (job hopping)*
- *Technological Savviness*
- *Collaboration (flat hierarchies)*
- *Feedback and recognition*

- *Diversity and inclusion*
- *Corporate social values*
- *Entrepreneurial spirit*

Millennials' views on work reflect their adaptation to a rapidly changing world, emphasizing personal fulfillment, flexibility, and social impact alongside traditional career goals. As this generation increasingly becomes the most influential population in the workforce, their values and preferences are significantly influencing workplace cultures and employment trends worldwide.

Are you prepared to work with a Millennial? The key characteristics of a Millennial work style are swift, efficient, tech savvy, and results oriented. They earn the respect of their colleagues and leaders through relationships and actions, not by role/title. You will have to prove yourself to a Millennial. They will follow, support, and work with you only if they respect you. A Millennial might say, "We are not here at work to have a good time, we are here to get work done, so we can have a good time after work."

Boomers are managing, Gen Xers are driving, Millennials are doing the work.

Generation Z

Building skill, gaining knowledge, and experimenting in their careers.

Generation Zers were born between 1997–2010. Their outlook on work reflects a blend of pragmatic and aspirational goals that are shaped by the unique socio-economic environment they've grown up in, including global challenges such as climate change and the COVID-19 pandemic. The amount of Gen Zers in the workforce is more than half the number of Millennials and about the same as the number of Baby Boomers. For this young generation, selecting a career, an industry, a company, or a job is complex.

I have a few Gen Z mentees, and we spend most of our time talking about building necessary skills and exploring long-term career and life goals. Gen Z employees can sense alignment with their organization quickly. Do they believe in their mission, do leaders honor their organization's values, and is my manager here to help me? Most Gen Z employees are in their early career lifecycle stages: Acquire or Develop (Chapter 4). In these stages, employees are building skill and knowledge and experimenting in their careers. Don't be concerned if you are a Gen Zer and you have multiple jobs.

Building confidence is a critical need for most Gen Zers. This generation is seeking success but they have not yet had the life experiences to judge what it takes. On the other hand, Gen Zers are growing up in a complex time, with many opportunities and many challenges. This is the first generation to see being an "influencer" as a career, and the first to see a truly global workforce, where programmers and big data work can be performed throughout the world.

They seek flexibility, experiences, and a career-life balance that challenges all previous generations.

Here are some of the key perspectives and values around work that characterize Gen Z:

- *Purpose-driven work*
- *Work-life balance*
- *Empathy, not authority*
- *Professional development*
- *Technological integration (digital natives)*
- *Authenticity and transparency*
- *Diversity and inclusion*
- *Opportunity and variety (gig economy)*
- *Flexibility and autonomy*
- *Feedback and recognition*

Companies looking to attract and retain Gen Z talent will need to consider these values and expectations. A company's vision, mission, and values will drive Gen Z employees toward or away from the company or the industry. In addition, the use of technology will positively attract potential Gen Z employees.

This generation can be frustrating to employers but it represents the future workforce. Take an opportunity to find and grow future leaders and dedicated employees. Most employee turnover occurs within this age group, and it is understandable. This generation of employees is just beginning to build their careers and find their aspirations. Maybe the realities of life have changed things. Maybe an industry, a company, or a new role is not what was expected. Employers and employees have a real opportunity to explore the fit, and begin a long - lasting partnership. But most employers do not take the time necessary to build partnerships with their Gen Z employees.

Purpose drives value, performance reflects value.

Generation Alpha

How will we work in the future?

The newest workplace generation is Generation Alpha and includes those born between approximately 2010–2025. Characteristics of Gen Alpha are still emerging, as this generation is barely in the workforce. As Gen Alpha continues to grow up, generational characteristics, preferences, and societal impact will emerge. They will likely be the most technologically integrated generation, continuing to shape significant cultural change and promoting social and environmental agendas in the decades to come.

Leverage technology and productivity.

Summary

Understanding the workforce and employee expectations are critical to creating a sustainable organization. Arguably, all organizations need to ensure that generational differences are understood and embraced. Creating the employer and employee value proposition is key to employee retention and sustainable cultures.

Recognizing the generational differences within an organization is an important first step in creating a more collaborative workforce. Acknowledge that priorities and viewpoints change over time. Generations work differently, communicate differently, and value different things from their careers and lives.

Generations in the Workforce

- *Baby Boomers (1946–1964):* Following their mantra of "Work hard, keep your head down, and you will get what you deserve"

- *Generation X (1965–1980):* Driving organizational results while trying to connect Baby Boomers and Millennials

- *Millennials (1981–1996):* Doing the work and always looking for more challenge and opportunity

- *Generation Z (1997–2010):* Building skill and knowledge, while experimenting with their careers

- *Generation Alpha (2010–2025):* The newest workforce, leveraging technology, experimenting with the

> *gig economy, and finding a passion that can make money*

Honor the differences in career and life expectations. Know what yours are.

CHAPTER 3

Generational Bias

"The greatest of all art is the art of living together." – Pablo Picasso

Embrace generational difference in career and life values.

As a Baby Boomer, I have found a new life passion of sticking up for the Millennial and Gen Z employees. Whether it is in a business meeting or sitting around a campfire, younger generations are accused of some pretty horrible things: never talking on the phone (just texting), finding answers on the Internet, and the worst of all, working from home or remotely.

You're kidding, right?

My view is that younger employees are more productive, more creative, and more accountable than ever before. It is different now, we must find new ways of measuring successful communication and work productivity, and the diligence of research and critical thought. Why do we have to concern ourselves with the way things were and not focus on how things can be better?

Managers, here's the thing. Not everyone looks at their careers or life as you look at yours. As a foundation, generational differences exist regarding what employees want from their careers. Of course, not everyone fits into these generational stereotypes, but appreciating a potential bias is important. How many times do you hear the following about the newer generations in the workforce?

- *Don't work hard*
- *Aren't loyal*
- *Don't respect authority*
- *Are job hoppers*
- *Need constant recognition*

Some of these observations are true, but many are just a reflection of how generational views differ in the workplace. The trick as a manager is to recognize what motivates your employees and then provide them with an environment where they value their work and can find ways to partner with you and the company to create a meaningful career and life.

Understanding these general tendencies can help foster intergenerational communication and collaboration. It's also crucial for employers to recognize the diverse needs and strengths of different generational cohorts to create a more inclusive, creative, and productive work environment.

My observations on generational bias are seen through my interactions with organizations and my mentees and colleagues. Partnering with a career requires you to understand your partners, adapt and have a little fun by celebrating our differences.

Cross-Generational Framework

As I mentioned before, I like simplifying complexity. As I have worked with my mentees, I've found a few career expectations that have evolved and will continue to evolve across generations. There are no certainties in this framework, but I hope you find it helpful in understanding some of the differences that exist in the workplace.

Many of our expectations have formed from observing the generation ahead of us, learning from them and adjusting our own views of career and life. There are many new opportunities to explore as we build our careers and lives, and that's why it's so important that we take charge and drive our desired outcomes. Why? Corporate loyalty to their employees has vanished. There is an increasing global, competitive labor market and social and economic pressures have required straight forward and deliberate action by both employers and employees.

I have built a Cross-Generational Framework to help clarify the unique views and expectations of the generations currently in the workforce. The premise of this book is to find ways to partner with your career to build the life you desire. Part of this process is building relationships with leaders, managers, and colleagues that will support you in your career and your life.

There are six generational workplace expectations to help explain how you might build partnerships in the workplace to advance your career and achieve your life goals.

CROSS GENERATIONAL FRAME WORK

☐	CONTROL VS FLEXIBILITY	☑
☑	COMMITMENT TO COMPANY VS COMMITMENT TO SELF	☐
☑	SHARE VALUE VS SOCIAL VALUE	☐
☐	DIGIT VS DIGITAL	☑
☐	PATIENCE VS IMPATIENCE	☑
☑	AUTHORITY VS EMPATHY	☐

Control vs. Flexibility

Flexibility is a key for engaging and motivating Gen Zers.

Having control of their work and those processes and systems available to make work efficient are welcomed by all employees. But what if the available systems are outdated and are primarily in place to manage and monitor performance? Gen Zers in particular repel systems that make work more difficult, that create unnecessary "noise," and that are not supportive of their assignments. A prime example in today's organizations is the balance between spending time updating a Client Relationship Management system or spending time with clients. Managers do need pipeline and sales forecasts, so some sort of tracking is necessary, but control for control's sake is seen as a waste of time for many Millennials and Gen Zers. If management and control systems are put into place, their value should be clearly demonstrated to the organization.

Flexibility is a key for engaging and motivating younger employees. Millennials and Gen Zers want to choose how and where they do their work. The old paradigm of having colleagues down the hall to speak with—to collaborate or chitchat with—are not important to newer work teams. Technology has offered us many opportunities to communicate, collaborate, and build relationships without physically being together. Allow Gen Zers the flexibility to create the working environment in which they are most productive.

This is not to suggest that face-to-face interaction is irrelevant. It is certainly reasonable for employers to require collaboration in person but have a clear purpose. Many organizations believe they need their employees together in order to build a positive company culture. If that is the case, make those interactions truly meaningful and beneficial. A key message should be "we can do more together than apart," so let's support each other in achieving our individual and team goals. Also remember, organizational culture is driven by the behaviors and actions of the leaders, not whether people are in the same physical space.

Flexibility is an asset in the workplace. It allows us to explore new assignments, it provides teachable moments, and it fosters self-determination. Control has its place, too. An analogy that works for me is to think of control and flexibility like the yellow and white lines on our roadways.

Yellow lines are there for our safety, white lines are there to guide us. Be sure you understand the yellow lines in your organization and use the white lines to advise you on the path forward.

Yellow lines for safety, white lines to guide you.

Commitment to Company vs. Commitment to Self

Commitment is your greatest gift!

Commitment is one of your greatest gifts. Use It wisely! How do you use your commitment? Organizations generally associate commitment with support of the corporate vision and mission, behaviors aligned with the core values, and accountability to deliver on your assignments.

Evaluating your commitment to your organization is difficult. An organization should honor you by providing you with development opportunities and keep you engaged in the future direction of the organization. Committing to your work is important. We do best when we are committed!

The psychological contract you are making with your organization needs to be clear. What are your assignments and what are your expectations? As a manager, one of your primary objectives is to clearly define assignments for your team members. Define what support you can provide and how success will be measured. As an employee, if you are not clear what your primary assignments are or how you will be measured, find out NOW!

Beyond completing assignments, supporting your organization's vision, mission, and core values are critical. Above all, this will define your fit in the organization. If you are committed to the organization's strategic direction, you should expect meaningful work and opportunities to grow your career. If you cannot support the organization's strategic direction and culture, you need to find another organization or company. Don't waste your time reconciling your dilemma unless you are in a position to change the culture.

So where should your commitment lie? Your organization has an opportunity to extend a value proposition to support your career and your life. Are they being successful? If not, the ball is in your court. Let's talk about commitment to self. The younger you are, the less likely you have seen organizations commit to their employees. Culture and markets are moving fast, companies and organizations need to be agile. Millennials and Gen Zers need to navigate their careers and lives in an ever-changing environment. It is not a "selfish self" who does this; it is a "necessary self!" A necessary self is one who has defined goals and is determined to develop a career path that supports those goals.

It's not "selfish self," but "necessary self!"

Share Value vs. Social Value

Are you delivering social and environmental benefits?

I began writing this book in Sintra, Portugal, and have escaped to Cadiz, Spain, to finish it. I have been fortunate enough to accumulate enough financial wealth that allows me to work in locations where I can write my books most effectively. Surprisingly, I always find ways to see the differences and the commonalities in life. While I am here In Spain, as with Portugal, you pay for your water, your bread and your olives at a restaurant. You have mass transportation to offer efficiencies in travel and you have a master key to control your homes electricity. The simplicity in life has crafted habits and rituals that support a less disruptive life.

In addition, I have spent my career in the environmental and engineering consulting industry. I have led teams to explore the development of Environmental and Social Governance (ESG) services and have had numerous discussions with clients on how they can develop a green brand. The goal was to find a balance between supporting the earth and building the business in realistic and achievable ways. For many of us, as individuals or corporations, this is a difficult balance to strike.

How committed is your organization to creating social and environmental benefits in your markets and for your employees? I've been on corporate leadership teams that do a day at the food shelter, take pictures and post them on LinkedIn. I've seen organizations promote volunteer efforts with their employees, but their individual expectations don't change. When you evaluate your company's brand and their commitment to a better world, don't fool yourself with these marketing gestures, it's the little things that make a difference. You should believe in your products, services and value you are adding to your communities you serve.

Does the organization you work with create shareholder value and social value? This is the question that many younger career developers are asking before and after they accept employment. An organization and its leadership are clearly accountable to its shareholders. The social value they create is not a must for them, but it may be to its prospective employees of the younger generation.

I feel that most industries can provide meaningful value to society and the environment. Key to this is in the way organizations realize the benefits they are contributing to society and the environment. As a business, the story you construct for your clients and employees must be aligned with your vision, mission, and core values. Baby Boomers and Gen Xers are vested in company benefits, and compensation plans are rewarded by growing shareholder value. Millennial and Gen Z employees may not be motivated by these longer-term incentive plans and resist the notion that their value is associated with corporate share value.

Millennials are a critical part of your organization. To retain them and attract valuable Gen Z employees, organizations must demonstrate the social and environmental benefits that are created by their products and services. Regardless of the industry, Millennial and Gen Z employees are looking for meaningful work with organizations that can demonstrate positive social and environmental benefits.

Find meaningful work.

Digit vs. Digital

Do we fear using our brains rather than our pencils?

It continues to surprise me, the lack of digital awareness we accept in the workplace. Digital solutions have been and can be developed for almost every aspect of our business, yet organizations have only just begun to develop productive relationships with technology and have not yet brought the value of technology to their customers, partners, and employees. Baby Boomers and some Gen Xers remain timid in their willingness to accept technology, generally fearing the changes that digital solutions will make to their business.

Moving to paperless solutions, for example, can build efficiencies and security that are not available through manual efforts. The benefits are clear, but for many reasons, the adoption of technology threatens the value we bring to the organization. Simple things can be done with technology, leaving the complexities of our solutions to us. Is that what we fear, using our brain rather than our pencils to advance our solutions?

So, if you are a Gen Zer, you were likely using a digital app through a smartphone or tablet before you were ten years old. Your fluency with technology is seemingly inherent to you. As I think about which hardware store I can by the DIY part I need, you have already ordered it on Amazon. Can you imagine waiting on your manager to solve a problem when a solution could be found from a Google search? How about building a marketing outline from scratch versus using Chat GPT to develop one?

Yes, this is the new work environment. Information and knowledge are available as you need it. We create value when we understand the solution our technology has provided us. We test it and confirm the effectiveness of the solutions we develop. We remain the ultimate translator between form and function. Millennials and Gen Zers come to work to be successful. They expect organizations to have efficient systems in place and to be asked to do the hard work, not the routine work that can be done digitally. Organizations that drive digital solutions will benefit their clients and their employees. For a traditional organization, this may mean changing your business model, your view of productivity, and your culture, but it will benefit your clients and employees if done right!

> **Digital solutions bring value to our clients, partners and employees.**

Patience vs. Impatience

> **Patience is a virtue, isn't it?**

We have been taught that "patience is a virtue." The origin of this phrase is a fifth century poem from the Latin poet Prudentius. Well, things have changed since the fifth century! The speed of life and work have accelerated and will likely accelerate more into the future. So why do we wait to make decisions, to make changes, or to gain the value we deserve?

Organizations have their tempos, unique rhythms that develop over time. Generally, smaller organizations tend to be nimbler and work at a faster pace compared to larger organizations, which can be more lethargic and slower to act.

Where do you fit?

Gen Xer have to find the organizational rhythm and play by the rules. They understand the yellow lines in the organization and may have to risk too much for violating its pace. Millennials are watching, measuring and advancing ideas and solutions based on their commitment to effect change and advance their own ideas. Gen Zers move to the pace of "why not now?" If my idea is a good one, why not move it forward right now. Why wait?

To accommodate, endorse, and support a change brought forth by a Millennial or Gen Zer affirms their value in the organization. The opposite will irritate and frustrate this newer generation of employees. Of course, not every idea is a good one, but organizations need to create learning environments that allow active engagement by younger staff to contribute their ideas about the business or the organization. I don't mean annual employee surveys here; I mean solutions that can help contribute to the organization's bottom line.

One other thing to touch on: This idea of the newbie saying, "I want to be CEO next year." Extreme career advancement expectations can be seen as overly ambitious, but motivation to excel is a positive attribute. If that's you, find an organization that wants to foster that in you. If you are a manager, be willing to coach your motivated employees. Many in the younger generations have not been exposed to knowledgeable career mentors. I speak to the importance of building an advisory team in **Own Your Career – No One Else Will**. Here, let's just say, give your younger employees a view of what it takes to be CEO, surround them with coaches and mentors. Teach them the necessary skills, give them challenging assignments, and keep them engaged in the strategic direction of the firm. If they don't become CEO in your organization, they might do so in your competitor's organization.

Affirm Millennial and Gen Zers by accepting change.

Authority vs. Empathy

If you do one thing, have empathy.

Let's talk about this one! Most Baby Boomer and Gen Xers have been raised in a culture where respecting management is paramount; they feel they have earned the right to boss you around. Seniority has its place, but it is no longer enough. Every manager and every colleague I have worked with has earned my trust. I think that is the way things work today, with trust. There is no immediate acceptance of authority based on title or reporting relationship.

Earning trust is not something everyone learns how to do. It is difficult, but it is worth pursuing. There are a lot of ways to earn someone's trust: be honest, do what you say you will do, and work to build a strong relationship. Trust does not come easy; it can be painful and require a lot of work. A client of mine once told me, "Paul, I will not trust you unless we have been through some hard times together." We had many ups and downs together, and he became a mentor of mine. My lesson learned: If you do one thing, have empathy! With empathy, trust grows.

Your teams and your colleagues face many challenges in the workplace and outside the workplace. To successfully lead your team, you must understand what motivates them and how you can support them. Remember the different generations. Baby Boomers and Gen Xers have likely compartmentalized their anxieties and concerns, and they may be in positions of authority. Millennials and Gen Zers are earning their stripes, proving their value to the organizations.

If you are a manager, how will you exercise your authority? And how will you, as an employee, communicate your needs for success? These are conversations that occur between partners, those who have mutual goals and share a common desire to help each other.

Don't be that "hard ass!" Understand that you needed a break, too!

Summary

Whether you are working with your clients, colleagues, or team, recognize how you might be able to more effectively communicate and work together. In many ways, the workplace should be a straightforward environment: Most organizations have either a product or a service to deliver to their clients. The complication arises in that the workplace requires the collaboration of cross-generational teams that perceive their jobs, their careers, and their lives differently.

Cross-Generational Framework

- ✓ **Control vs. Flexibility:** *Flexibility in the workplace allows employees to choose their most productive environments to execute on their clearly defined assignments.*

- ✓ **Commitment to Company vs. Commitment to Self:** *Individually, our ability to commit is one of our greatest gifts. Keep clear your commitments to your organization and your commitments to yourself in support of your career and life goals.*

- ✓ **Share Value vs. Social Value:** *Organizations that demonstrate their environmental and social contributions attract employees who are aligned with their passions. Talk about value!*

- ✓ **Digit vs. Digital:** *Adopting digital tools to help us be more efficient allows us to create greater value in our ability to focus on new, enhanced, and higher-level solutions.*

- ✓ **Patience vs. Impatience:** *The speed of organizational change will either attract or repel employees, who want to be valued for meaningful contributions.*

- ✓ **Authority vs. Empathy:** *Authority comes through the trust built between manager and team. To build trust, choose the empathic path.*

Meaningful relationships allow you to be your most effective self and open the doors to true partnerships.

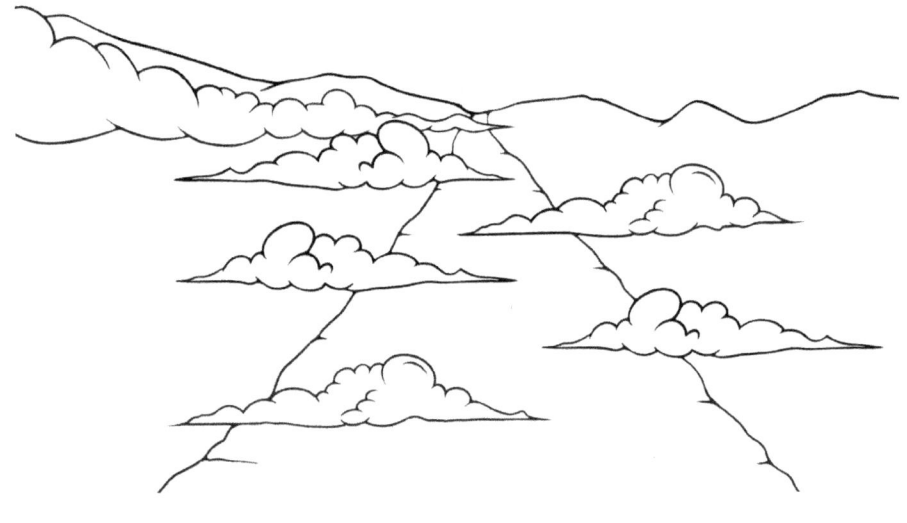

CHAPTER 4

A Career Shouldn't Be a Mystery

"In character, in manner, in style, in all things, the supreme excellence is simplicity."
— Henry Wadsworth Longfellow

Set your destination and keep looking forward.

Careers are all different, unique to you, though most of us travel a fairly common career lifecycle. During the writing of my first book, ***Own Your Career – No One Else Will,*** I interviewed several career developers across gender, age, and professions. What I found was the opportunity to build a Career Lifecycle Model that could describe the career journey of many. I wanted the model to be easy, definable, and have simple language that could be used with career developers, their managers, and their mentors. I have tested the model over the last few years. As with any model, it does not fit all career journeys, but it may fit yours. Within five minutes of talking to someone, I can describe to them their current career lifecycle stage, what to expect, and how to prepare for their next stage.

Developing a career aspiration is part of the ADAPT Career Lifecycle Model. A key part of a journey is having a destination. A career aspiration keeps you looking forward and gives you tangible measures of success. I find that about 80% of my mentees have a career aspiration in mind but have not taken the time to write it down, challenge it, review it routinely, and make adjustments when life changes.

Sometimes your career unfolds sort of naturally or around you, and that's OK. If you want your career to happen to you, fine. Take care to recognize when opportunities develop and stay engaged in building a lifetime of challenges and experiences. One of my mentees said to me, "I follow my heart and make enough money to live." Another mentee noticed that "What you think you will do is likely not what you will be doing in ten years." The way I look at a career is like a book. You will likely have many chapters over a forty-year journey. Your aspirations will change with time. However, it is always helpful to keep looking forward.

Use the ADAPT Career Lifecycle Model to map your journey.

Career Aspirations

Experiment, narrow, and accomplish.

A career aspiration is more than just answering the question, "What are you going to do when you grow up?" An employee's career aspiration is uniquely theirs. As an employee, you should not rely on others to define your ambitions. It is natural to see others in their careers and think, "If only I could do as well as they are doing." Don't be tempted to try to replicate their path. You should learn from others' experiences but take care to craft the career aspiration that best fits you.

You will also be the one who determines if your career ambition has been achieved. Know what it means to have achieved your career ambition. For example, I feel strongly that achieving a particular job title should not be a career ambition. Rarely do titles speak to challenges and successes.

So, how do you define your aspirations? Try to visualize the end of your career and what you want to have accomplished at that time. Is your ambition ultimately to own your own business? Maybe you want to make a lot of money and retire early. Whatever this visualization is, something it is not is a one-time snapshot. It is ongoing. Yes, write your career ambition down and look at it once a year. Are you on track and does it feel good? If so, great. But maybe that ambition no longer fits. Your career goals may change, and that is perfectly OK. The point is that you want to remind yourself of the journey you are on, and confirm that you are on the right path.

Recently, a cohort of young career developers had this to say about their career aspirations:

> *"I will have a career that aligns with my passions and values, while allowing me to retire at age sixty."*
>
> *"I will be valued by my peers as a dependable member of the team. My career will inspire me, and I will be fairly compensated."*
>
> *"I will have a career that is rewarding, builds relationships, and provides me financial comfort."*

> *"[To] work hard, leverage my skills, and live a life I want."*
>
> *"I want to be fulfilled by my career and enjoy the people I work with."*

I have to admit that I did not have a career aspiration until the last fifteen years of my career. I was fortunate to be in a rapidly growing industry with plenty of opportunities for career development. My early career lifecycle stages, including my Develop and Apply stages (discussed below), were a whirlwind. I was fortunate to have people supporting and believing in me. My career aspiration started on a Delta Airlines napkin on a long trip from Amsterdam to Minneapolis. It was simply doodles and a list of things I wanted to accomplish before I ended my career. It included how I wanted to finish my career, when I was going to retire, and what I would do after retirement. I kept this napkin for many years until I copied it to a page in my work journals. Yes, it helped; I still have a copy of it in my desk.

Allow me to share with you the ADAPT Career Lifecycle Model and some example career aspirations that could resonate based on where you are in your career journey.

Your career aspiration is unique to you. Own it.

The ADAPT Career Lifecycle Model

The ADAPT Career Lifecycle model is simple, providing a common language to set goals and assess opportunities.

The workplace is certainly more complicated these days than ever before, but it also brings great opportunities. The traditional approach to developing a career—finding a predictable career track—is less common. Today, you can invent your own career track. The opportunity to break out of the pack with a great idea, product, or service seems boundless. Regardless of your approach though, the ADAPT Career Lifecycle Model can help you continually navigate your career journey.

The ADAPT (Acquire, Develop, Apply, Produce, and Transition) Career Lifecycle Model is designed to support individual career development from start to finish. The model also allows you to start again and again. There are no ages, no durations, and no must dos. No preferred career tracks. Every career is unique, runs on its own continuum, and requires your input every step along the way.

While the model's stages may look linear, meaning you must complete the first stage before moving to the next, they are not. Most of the interviews I have completed, and mentees I have coached, come back to an early career lifecycle stage after redefining their career aspirations.

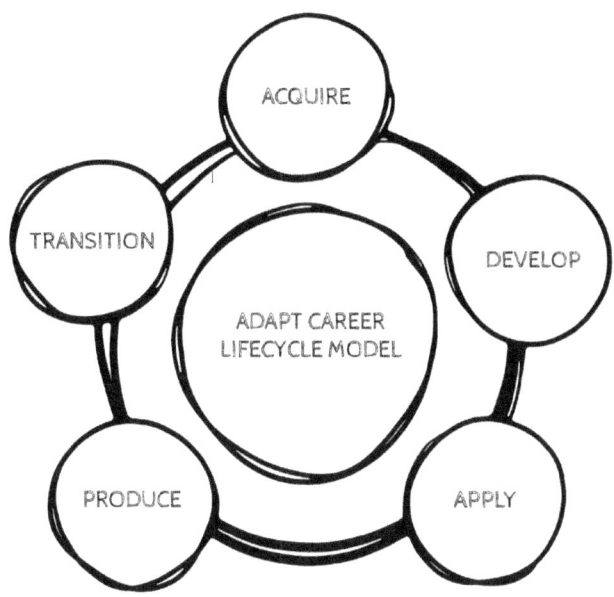

So, let's look at the five stages.

Acquire

Acquire is the first stage of your career lifecycle. This stage includes experimentation and the brainstorming of ideas on how to build the foundation of your career. It encourages you to be open-minded and to seek knowledge. It also teaches you the basic skills needed to be a contributing member of a work team or company.

Generally, this stage happens at the beginning of your career or when you choose to reinvent your career. You may not have a specific career in mind when you start but you can take the time to narrow your interests and seek knowledge.

This experience is different for everyone. We all come from different backgrounds. Your family and friends will be strong influencers and they may urge you down paths that don't fit your true passions. Don't be afraid to trust your instincts, to alter your route, and to expand your interests and your view of the world. You may choose formal education, apprenticeships, or the school of hard knocks.

However you proceed, you'll learn some basic skills and habits in your Acquire stage that will set you up for future success. This stage will require investment—emotionally and financially. Don't be reluctant to invest in yourself!

ASPIRATION 1: Follow Your Passion

Your aspirations will change throughout your career. Initially your aspirations may be quite broad and influenced by your life passion. As you develop your career, you will begin to balance your passions with your career and your life.

When you begin your career, you likely won't know exactly what you want to do or be able to visualize your ultimate career goal. That's OK! It is not easy to specifically define your career aspiration, so take it step by step. As you begin acquiring skills and knowledge, you will have many opportunities, some of which you did not anticipate. You may begin to see more specifically what you would like to build your career around. This is not an exact

science, so challenge yourself to see all your opportunities and craft a career aspiration that fits you.

Forming your career aspiration can take many forms. Some may be quite concrete: "I want to be an electrical engineer working in aerospace in France." Others may be less specific: "I would like to help people to improve their health and welfare."

Again, your aspiration may change with time, so there are no wrong answers. Define those things you can now and fill in the blanks as you develop your career.

Invest in yourself.

Develop

Develop is the second stage of your career lifecycle. It is when you take your skills and knowledge to the workplace. Maybe the job is not within your ultimate career, and likely it is not. Still, this stage allows you to gain confidence and practice the skills you have acquired. This is a period of uncertainty, a time when you are gaining your financial independence and learning about the frustrations of getting (and having) a job.

You also are building your collegial networks and looking for your first career break. You will be persistent, and you will be successful. You will be faced with deciding on your first job. The job may not be ideal, may not match your model of what you want to do, and will likely not pay what you expect. Don't fret; a startup job can help you continue to formulate your career aspirations and give you real-life work experience.

Start exploring the workplace, companies, institutions, or trades. You may find yourself changing jobs, roles, or industries to find the right fit for you. That's perfectly OK. You may also find that you would like to develop new skills and return to the Acquire stage. This may also be when you start to feel pressure to balance your career with your personal life. You are making new friends, changing cities, and becoming an independent adult. Financially, you can start to pay back some of your career investments: college loans and the like. Start small, if necessary, but start now.

ASPIRATION 2: Narrow Your Journey

As you begin your work and feel you are on your way, you can look at your career with a more realistic, and potentially, a more critical eye. Workplace experiences will help you refine your career aspiration. Let yourself be available to numerous assignments and duties. The key in the Develop stage is to assess how your passions can be translated to a successful career. Use your new insights to define the type of career you desire.

Start by capturing your desired outcomes and all the accomplishments you most hope to achieve during your career. Write them down.

Some inspiration:

"I think I would like my own clinic. That would allow me to develop a reputable medical practice, helping as many patients as possible."

"I would like to be recognized by my peers as an industry leader."

"I want to be a millionaire by age thirty-five."

"I feel compelled to make a significant contribution to enhancing health and advancing health equity."

"I seek to be a leader in a global company."

"The most important things are to support my family and have a meaningful and fulfilling career."

"I want to make meaningful change in the lives of people in need."

These aspirations may seem still too broad, but developing a career aspiration statement like these can provide some tangible boundaries to your career and help direct you forward.

Lastly, assess your skills and knowledge. Are they enough to fulfill your aspiration? You could be met with some hard decisions during this time. Ask yourself, "Do I have the right experience or training?" Challenge yourself to go back to school or further your experiences before moving on. These are aspirational statements, and they are meant to be on the horizon—your destination after many years of hard work. At this stage, time is on your side.

> Continue to define your aspiration and get real-life work experience.

Apply

The Apply stage of your career lifecycle is when you take your skills and knowledge to your preferred industry, company, or institution. You will start to see a longer career window. This stage helps you test, stretch, and confirm that you are on the right path. You are learning what you do well—and what you don't do well. Embrace your strengths and your weaknesses because understanding both are important as you develop your career.

This is also a critical time for developing your professional network, your industry/professional knowledge, and to begin building relationships with customers and key stakeholders. Don't underestimate the importance of these professional relationships. They are crucial to building strong, positive connections that will serve you well, long into the future.

This stage of your career may offer you the greatest challenge in how you manage your career pace. How quickly or slowly are you building your career? You may be on a scenic route or an expressway, or something in between. You choose. Ideally, this stage will also allow you to pay off your educational debt and focus on your financial future.

ASPIRATION 3 - Pick Your Destination and Your Path to It

You are likely becoming very focused on your career. You are working with those who challenge and teach you. You may also see your "like" person ("I want to be like Alicia or Derek."). You see successful people around you. You also see those who are merely putting in the time and counting the days. (I suspect that if you're reading this book, you're not counting the days. You are committed to growing your career and expect to do well!)

You are now taking small but important steps in your career. Given the number of opportunities you have, picking your ultimate destination may be difficult. Maintain connections with those who have supported you and believed in you. This social capital will help you as you grow your career.

Some key questions you should ask in this stage of your career include:

Am I in a growth industry? Does the industry align with my values and my desired life work?

Will my current company support me in achieving my professional and personal goals?

> **What other roles do I desire?**
>
> In addition, confirm or challenge the aspirational statements you made in the Develop stage. Do they remain relevant? Do they align with your passions and your life goals? Are they achievable? Maybe you have an updated career aspiration. Wonderful! Now take the necessary time to further articulate your ambitions.

Align your industry, your company, and your roles.

Produce

The Produce stage can be challenging but it is also the most rewarding. Here, you will need to run hard, fast, and possibly long, to achieve your fullest potential. Your career has a finite duration, likely forty to forty-five years, and you should make the most of it. Hopefully at this stage you have achieved your full career potential. It's a time when you are proud of your accomplishments and have largely met your career ambitions.

You may also feel more alone than ever because you're in charge. You may be leading a team, a business, or your own company. These can be lonely roles. Ask yourself who you turn to for advice, how do you communicate most effectively, and what lasting mark you want to make. At the risk of sounding morbid, this is when you begin to write your career eulogy.

The expectations of you in the workplace and at home can be significant during this time. You will need to find ways to keep your batteries charged and remain focus on what really matters. Maybe most importantly, your judgments and behaviors will create lasting impacts on the organization and your career. Again, there are no fixed durations or ages in this model, but this is when you should commit to fully accomplishing your career ambitions. It's also a time to accumulate wealth. That sounds self-serving, but trust me, financial flexibility is critical. So, develop and stay on a wealth-accumulation plan.

ASPIRATION 4: Seize the Moment

By now you are well on your way to achieving your career aspirations. You have narrowed your focus, built your career road map, and are entrenched on your career path. Your desired ambitions may be met by now. Challenge yourself to achieve your best and build a legacy you can be proud of. Put yourself at the end of your career and ask yourself, "Did I have a career, and a life well lived?"

Defining a successful career is more than having a strong and clear career aspirations. As you suspect, it is much more difficult than that. Define your life and career goals clearly and assess your progress routinely. As mentioned earlier, a successful career can support your life and help fulfill your life goals.

Be bold and seek opportunities to advance your career. You deserve every opportunity that presents itself to you. Cement your personal and professional brand and develop your own leadership style. Your colleagues are important, so support those who have supported you.

It is natural to question if you are in the right place for the end of your career. Your view of your career may be changing. On the other hand, you may be fully satisfied with the people you work with and the benefits you bring to the community and your family.

Either way, ask yourself, "What else can I achieve or do that will help others?" This may be volunteering, running for a public office, or coaching your favorite sport. It can be argued that such examples are not career-related, but they can lead to more satisfaction at work or at home.

> Your career journey has been hard work. Honor yourself by achieving all your career and life aspirations.

Transition

Transition is the fifth stage and is a time when you transition out of your career and/or create a new career or lifestyle. The most challenging part of this phase is the "when." When do you begin winding down your career or take the chance to reinvent yourself? When do you choose to leave the workforce? Should you have a retirement party or a startup party? A significant controlling factor will be your financial flexibility. By this time, your finances should be sound, allowing you to pursue a variety of options. That is the position you want to be in.

This period of your life can be very exciting but remember that you will need time to transition into it. It may be important for you to stay relevant, engaged, and interested in those things you found meaningful in your career. Or, you may want to completely leave the work world and make time for yourself and family. You may want to start a new career. Be thoughtful and proactive about your next steps and develop a personal plan to achieve your desired outcomes.

ASPIRATION 5: Feeling Satisfied, But What's Next?

Maybe the term "career aspiration" at this stage of your career is a misnomer. Maybe a better way to look at it is, "Am I satisfied?" If yes, think about what is next. Considering these questions while you are employed can be challenging. Finding the time to renew life goals, build a new business plan, or refine your financial plan takes time. Stay diligent in protecting the time you need to consider all your options.

To be realistic, you may also be considering how much time you really have. We would all like to live to be one hundred, but the chances of that are not in our favor. The time you have left no longer seems endless, and you no longer feel as invincible as you likely did in your twenties or thirties. You may have fulfilled your career ambition, but have you fulfilled your life's ambition yet?

Step back, take inventory of your career and life, and be selfish with your time. If you are still young or interested in starting a business, develop a business plan. If you are interested in retiring, develop a retirement plan. Regardless of the path you take, keep your life goals in front of you and take on the world.

Retire or reinvent, just do it on your terms.

Summary

Understanding your career aspirations as related to your career lifecycle stage can lead to the right discussions with your manager, partner, and colleagues. In addition, developing the big-picture view of your career and your life will help you prioritize the important activities in both.

What career lifecycle stage are you in?

- *Acquire:* Open-minded knowledge-seeking; experimenting with your career path

- *Develop:* Refining your career aspiration and developing confidence in the workplace

- *Apply:* Building your professional brand, networking, and fostering client relationships

- *Produce:* Reaching your career aspirations and leaving a lasting impact on your organization and people

- *Transition:* Moving on; retire or reinvent, just do it on your own terms

Based on my coaching and mentoring, I have found that career developers are distributed across the ADAPT Career Lifecycle Model. Regardless of the stage. It is important to recognize the stage you are in, to learn as much as you can, and then move on to your next career lifecycle stage.

Staying on your desired career track is quite an accomplishment. You will face numerous challenges as you do this while also building your life. I would like to invite you now to think about how you will partner with your career to create the life you deserve. Let's dig into the Career-Life Partnering Model!

Please feel free to visit my website www.PaulGoudreault.com to see all the Career Tidbits created for my first book, ***Own Your Career – No One Else Will.*** These tidbits are designed to either help you in your current role or help you move to your next career lifecycle stage.

A career aspiration keeps you looking forward and gives you tangible measures of success.

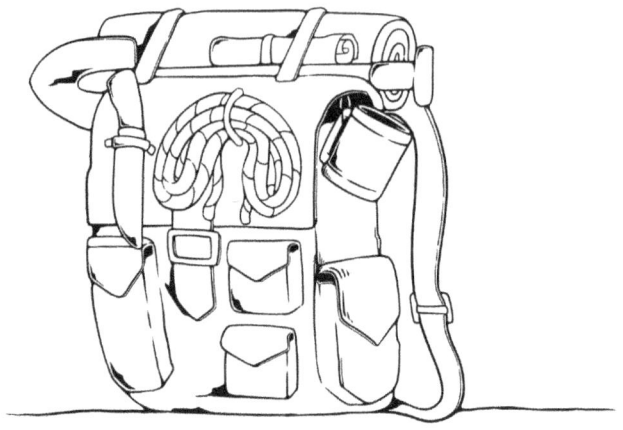

CHAPTER 5

Career-Life Partnering Model

"The strength of the team is each individual member. The strength of each member is the team." – Phil Jackson

Why Partnering?

Don't look for balance, look for good partners.

"How do I balance my career and my life?" This is a good question. A better question is, "How do I partner with my career to have the life I want?" I often think about my career and my life. Can I say they were always in balance? Certainly, no! However, I always knew that what I was doing with my career gave me the opportunity to live the life I wanted. I found myself spending too much time away from my family, eating too much, working too hard and stressing out about what I needed to do next for my clients or my company. Was it worth it, yes. I was treated fairly by my employer, challenged to develop myself both professionally and personally, and was able to build wealth for my family.

Both balancing and partnering are dynamic systems. They will change with time and require continued attention. It is fortunate for us that life never stays the same; how boring if it did. Balancing can commonly be done individually, by yourself. Your "system" is in equilibrium: the distribution of time, energy, and attention are equal. You can control how you use your time, your energy, and what you do with your passion. However, creating a meaningful career and purposeful life requires your ability to engage, develop, and build relationships. Do you consider your career a partner, and does this partner support your life's ambition?

Unlike balancing, which can be done alone, partnering requires, well, a partner. Partnering refers to collaboration, mutual benefits, and shared accountabilities. Unlike balance, partnering is not a solo venture. Can you truly balance your career and life without a partner or partners? Likely no. Partnering with your career, your workplace, your family and your friends will help you see that you can have a career that supports your life's ambitions. Partnering can be difficult; its success is heavily dependent on the compatibility and cooperation between the partners.

Balance is about maintaining equilibrium within or among various elements, often individually, while partnering is about joining forces with others to achieve common objectives. To me, partnering is the right way of thinking about how your career and life work together to provide you a career and life well lived. Create a world where your career is your friend, not your foe. Your manager is a colleague, not just your boss. Your organization should be a source of energy, not something that consumes you. Imagine coming to work every day knowing that you are getting as much from your career as you are giving.

Don't go it alone.

Career Isn't a Bad Word

Your career does not have to look like anyone else's. Make yours meaningful to you.

Today, there are many more opportunities to be self-employed, to work for multiple companies, or to start a business of your own. Think about where you are today. Are you developing a career or just working? How will you feel after twenty or thirty years of working? Careers are developed over time and as with anything that develops over time, a lot can go well, and a lot can go not so well. This is a good time to define your expectations for your career and your life, evaluate your progress and make any course correction while you still have time. I urge you not to wait until the end of your career to determine how well you have done creating a career and life well lived. Afterall, if you are lucky, you may get a retirement party. But, don't count on it!

As I speak with my mentees and young career developers, they hesitate to use the word "career." As if it's a bad word! In some cases, I hear:

> *"I don't have a career and don't need one."*
>
> *"I am fine working at what I do and really don't want to work my butt off for a company."*
>
> *"I'll be a TikTok influencer and life will be good."*
>
> *"Careers are for old people; I am young and don't need to figure that out now."*
>
> *"I don't want to work my whole life and not have a life to show for it."*

My first response is, "You will have a career whether you like it or not." My second response is, "You have an opportunity to define your career. Why not take ownership?" The years you will spend working will be the biggest investment in time and effort you will make during your life. Your time at work will surpass the time you spend with family, with friends, or in developing your passions in life.

Defining a career should be done on your own terms. Unfortunately, we are often judged for our careers. When I was CEO, people would ask me what my job was. I would start by describing what I did, what my degree was in, and who I worked for. When I mentioned that I was a CEO, I would see their view of me changing, for good or for bad! Defining your career aspiration and setting achievable goals along the way will help you create a career of your choosing. Don't judge your career against others. Allow yourself the freedom to explore your passions, develop yourself, and achieve both your career and life goals. What you choose to do with your career is up to you and no one else!

Like it or not, you will have a career.

Introducing the Career-Life Partnering Model

Commit to enhancing both your career and your life.

Do I focus on my career or my life? The answer is you can do both! It is not easy to take the time that is necessary to evaluate the likelihood of your success in achieving your career or life aspirations, but it is essential. As I worked with my mentees, I saw the need to develop a simple model that can help people focus on what is important, leveraging their strengths and identifying the challenges they may have in their career and their life. I also recognized that the process of determining priorities in both career and life is ongoing. I encourage my mentees to build their own personalized assessment and action plan annually. Your relationship with your work and your career will be critical in how you view your happiness.

The Career-Life Partnering Model is based on a very simple concept: We give a tremendous amount of our energy to work, to building our careers. In return, the value of what we give to our career should allow us to achieve both our professional and life goals. Over a forty-five-year career, you will spend close to 12,000 eight-hour days working! Is there are any other single activity in your life where you spend more time? Sleeping does not count!

So, what is the Career-Life Partnering Model? The model has three primary components: 1) Career-Life Care Assessment, 2) Career-Life Partnering Matrix, 3) Career Life Partnering Plan

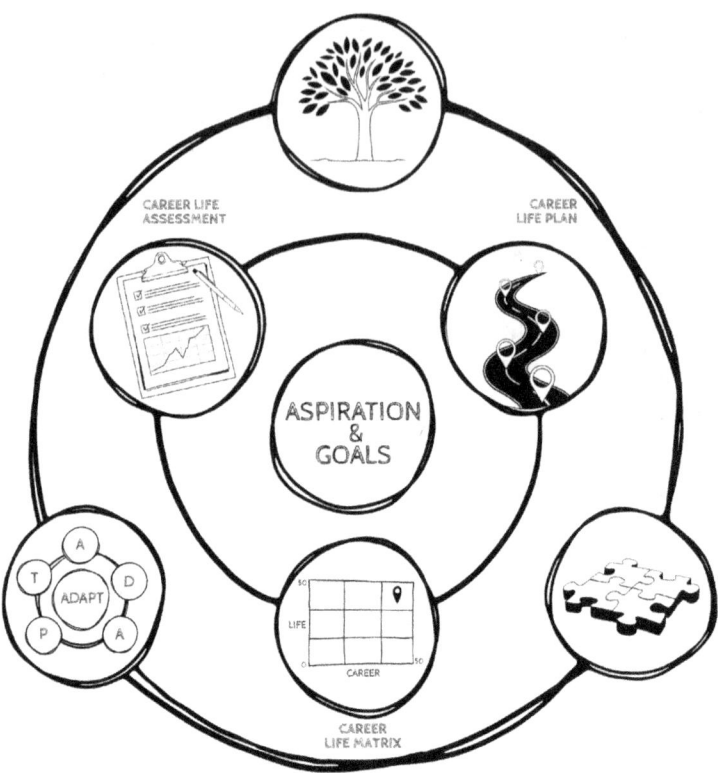

Let me share with you the general intent and desired outcomes of each of the Career-Life Partnering Model primary components. In the next chapters, we will dig into each component and provide you with sufficient information to conduct your very own evaluation and action plan.

The Career-Life Care Assessment (Chapter 6) has been developed for you to inventory your progress on the twenty Career and Life Building Blocks. These building blocks have been developed from my earlier book, **Own Your Career – No One Else Will,** and from my continued mentoring with my career developers. The assessment is the first step in clarifying where you might be today in striking a career-life partnership, including both your opportunities and your challenges.

It is critical to identify those things in your career and life that are going well and those that need some attention. These are your opportunities (leverage your strengths) and your challenges (areas needing attention). You will learn how to identify your opportunities and your challenges. As an example of what you might recognize, I have summarized recent comments from a coaching cohort that used the Career-Life Care Assessment to evaluate their current opportunities and challenges:

> *"I have a great advisory team and need to spend more time with them."*
>
> *"Sometimes I am timid in the workplace and can lose my confidence."*
>
> *"I am stressed out and life is too busy right now."*
>
> *"I have a strong work ethic and a strong desire to learn."*
>
> *"I am not spending enough time with my family and friends."*
>
> *"My partner and I need to spend more time working on developing our financial plan."*
>
> *"I need to become more deliberate at setting goals in my life and career."*
>
> *"My work colleagues are important to me, and I like working with them."*

As you assess your career and life needs, you can easily identify your top three opportunities and challenges for each. These opportunities and challenges begin to help you focus on the second part of the Career-Life Partnering Model.

Focus on what matters, now.

The Career-Life Partnering Matrix (Chapter 7) provides a summary of where you are on the path to a full partnership with your career. Are you living to work or working to live? You are likely somewhere in between the extremes. The matrix can provide insights on how to modify your actions to achieve your desired position at work and in life.

This second part of the Career-Life Partnering Model is looking at where you are in your career-life partnership. Based on your total ratings from each of your Career and Life Building Blocks, you can quickly assess where you are on your career-life partnering journey. Remember, partnerships are successful when they establish mutual benefits and accountabilities. So, ask yourself both what you give to your career and what you take from it. A partnership can only develop if the partners are clear on their expectations and commitments.

Let's use some specifics:

> *"I give my time, energy and knowledge."*
>
> *"I am dedicated to my work and I give it my full attention."*
>
> *"I am always connected to work and give my clients the highest level of care."*

"I take from work a sense of accomplishment & financial stability."

"I take pride in my relationships at work and I am encouraged about my career growth."

"I need to take time from work for my family & friends."

"I need to give more time in planning out my career."

"Right now, I can only give 40 hours a week to my career."

"I am looking to take my next step in my career."

As you reflect on your individual give and takes, be realistic and selfish. You will likely be able to identify your current career-life partnership as being in one of three primary stages:

- ◎ ***Informed:*** *You are aware of the Career and Life Building Blocks and ready to use them as you pursue your career-life partnership.*

- ◎ ***Enlightened:*** *You have begun developing the necessary behaviors in support of achieving your career or life goals. Prioritize and address the building blocks you deem appropriate.*

- ◎ ***Purposeful:*** *You have achieved the behaviors needed to reach your career or life goals. Selectively address the building blocks that help you sustain your desired outcomes.*

Now is the time to commit to those things that will allow you to move your career life partnership in the right direction.

Be realistic but be selfish and define your needs.

The Career-Life Partnering Plan (Chapter 9) is a tool you can use to map and define your next steps. The tough part of any journey is planning your itinerary. It is easy to pick a location and develop ideas on what you want to see and do. The tough part is figuring out how you will get to your locations and choose your venues along the way. Most of us do not travel solo, so you will have to accommodate your needs and preferences with those of others.

Building your plan is important. Managing to your plan is even more important. As with any plan, yours will need to be modified over time to capture the changes in your career and your life. For those who generally find little value in having a plan, do not skip this step. Instead, I suggest you develop a plan with just the level of detail that is consistent with your interest. Consider where you are today, where you want to be, and how you will map your journey.

Here are some of the considerations that can be included in your Career-Life Partnering Plan:

- *Your career aspirations and life goals*
- *Your current career lifecycle stage and your next*
- *Your next key roles, inside or outside of your organization*
- *Your top three career and life opportunities and challenges*

- *Your identified "gaps" (what you may have to obtain in order to meet your career ambition or life goals)*

- *Your assessment: What do you need from your career to help you achieve your life goals?*

The plan you build can also be used to help communicate your expectations to your organization, coaches, mentors, and partners. Be sure to measure your success and celebrate your accomplishments along the way. Take the time you need to create a plan that works for you!

Your life goals and your career aspirations will change over time, and so should the partnership between them.

Summary

The Career-Life Partnering Model seems a bit scientific, but it is not. The model evolved after working with a cohort of younger career professionals who wanted to learn more about how they could develop an action plan for both their careers and their lives. I resisted at first to quantify the requirements of a fulfilling career and a happy life. My single premise in my mentoring is that "you own your career and life; you define it and plan for it." As I continued to work with the cohort, I became convinced that we could arrive at some general building blocks to help us all navigate our career and life journeys.

> **The Career-Life Partnering Model**
>
> *The Career-Life Partnering Model has been developed to help you recognize the status of your current career-life partnership and to support you in defining your next steps. In the next chapters we will look at the:*
>
> - ✔ ***Career-Life Care Assessment:*** *Twenty Career and Life Building Blocks to help you assess your top opportunities and challenges in building a successful career-life partnership*
>
> - ✔ ***Career-Life Partnering Matrix:*** *A quick guide to illustrate where you might be on your career-life journey and what behaviors you can take to accelerate your career-life partnership.*
>
> - ✔ ***Career-Life Partnering Plan:*** *A simple roadmap to help you set your direction and identify milestones towards achieving your career-life partnership*

My request: Find what is helpful to you. Challenge your thinking about your career and your life. Build a team of advisors you admire and take your journey with your eyes wide open!

Treat your career as a partner in living the life you deserve.

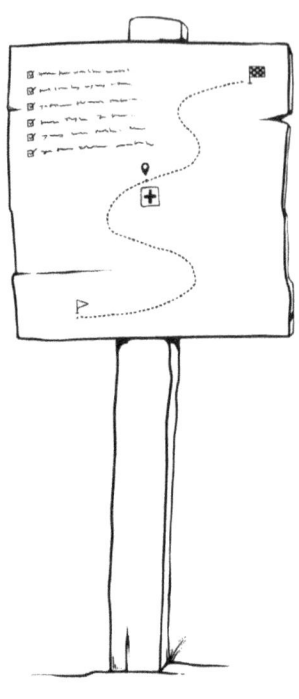

CHAPTER 6

Career-Life Care Assessment

"The time to repair the roof is when the sun is shining." – John F. Kennedy

Challenge yourself with those priorities you know are important for achieving your goals.

Your career aspiration and your career lifecycle are fairly predictable and can be managed by your behaviors and actions in the workplace. On the other hand, your life path is less predictable and will likely present many challenges as you travel your life path. If anything is certain, life is uncertain. Being proactive with your career and your life could help cut down the variability. If we choose not to plan, we choose others planning for us.

Is it possible to know all the things you need to address in order to have a successful career and life? Probably not. But you can challenge yourself with those priorities you know are important for achieving your goals. You can't just wake up in the morning and say to yourself, "I am going to be happy today." Happiness is achievable, and it will be the experiences, successes, and failures on the pursuit of happiness that will bring you the most joy.

So, in the context of pursuing happiness through experiences, guess where you spend the most time in the pursuit of happiness? You got it, with your work and with your partner/family and friends. This is why it is so important to look at your career as a partner in achieving happiness and a meaningful life. Your career should provide you with opportunities to create the life you deserve. If you find yourself "stuck," it is likely because you have not defined your priorities or are not focusing on what is important to you. Deciding what is most important and eliminating distractions may be the best way of getting unstuck.

Prior to digging into the Career-Life Partnering Matrix and the Career-Life Partnering Plan, let's look at how we can routinely evaluate our current career-life priorities. In Appendix I, you have a Career-Life Partnering Assessment; it is also available on my website (www.PaulGoudreault.com). Many of my mentees have used this assessment to gauge their progress in focusing on the most important priorities to move their career and life forward. The assessment is straightforward and is made up of three components:

- ◎ ***Career Care Assessment:*** *Ten career Building Blocks that are important to fully developing your career*

- ◎ ***Life Care Assessment:*** *Ten life Building Blocks that can guide you to a fulfilling life*

- ◎ ***Opportunities and Challenges:*** *Identify your priorities to leverage or enhance your success*

In total, you are presented with twenty building blocks that can provide you with the insights you may need to make necessary changes in both your career and life. Each building block describes an ideal position that, if obtained and maintained, should allow you to focus on behaviors that will enhance both your career and your life. The Career and Life Building Blocks have been developed through my coaching and mentoring and interviews completed with peers, colleagues, and friends.

For each building block, you will determine how well you have obtained the ideal position from *1 (Not so much) to 3 (In progress) to 5 (Absolutely nailed it).* This Is how you will evaluate your progress towards mastering the priorities that are important in developing your career-life partnership.

Your career should provide you with opportunities to create the life you deserve.

Career Care

Try to keep your career simple. Focus on what matters.

If you read my first book, **Own Your Career – No One Else Will**, you were introduced to 100 Tidbits. These tidbits are simple lessons on how to manage a successful career. They were each observed or taught to me along the way of my career, and I felt they would be helpful to other career developers. Over several years, I developed a list of "aha moments" while in meetings, talking to clients, participating in strategic planning, or visiting with colleagues. These "aha moments" turned into the 100 Tidbits!

The purpose of the tidbits is to provide practical examples on how you can enhance your career. As I worked with my mentees, I consolidated several of the tidbits and constructed the Career Building Blocks. These are what I thought were most important in developing a successful career. I encourage you to review all the Tidbits from ***Own Your Career – No One Else Will.*** There are many practical tips for advancing your career. The book is available on Amazon or by order at your local bookstore. Tidbit summaries are available at www.PaulGoudreault.com.

10 Career Building Blocks

1. *<u>Career Aspiration</u>: Developing a long-term vision for your career.*

   I have developed a long-term career aspiration that guides my career decisions. I review my aspiration annually to be sure it remains aligned with both my professional and my life goals.

2. *<u>Advisory Team:</u> Having a team to support you in your career and life.*

   I have assembled an advisory team that I can talk to about my career. My team includes internal and external mentors, coaches, therapist, doctors and/or a financial planner.

3. *<u>Investing in Yourself:</u> You are your most important asset; continually invest in yourself.*

   I routinely look for opportunities to advance my professional and educational knowledge through research, course studies, certifications, and conferences.

4. **_Career Plan:_** _A formalized action plan to achieve your career aspiration._

    I have a career plan that identifies my career opportunities over the next three to five years. My plan includes any gaps I need to fill to be positioned for my future roles. I review my career plan annually.

5. **_Networking Matters:_** _Having a network of industry professionals to explore opportunities._

    I actively identify and connect with professional relationships outside my advisory team that can help me understand my industry and potentially provide me future opportunities.

6. **_Organization:_** _Understanding your organization's direction and aligning your goals._

    I am aligned with my organization's culture and believe in its vision, mission, or purpose. I also believe that my organization will provide me with opportunities to achieve my career aspiration.

7. **_Professional Brand:_** _Having a positive and confident brand at work and with industry peers._

    I have developed a strong professional brand within my industry. My brand reflects positively on me and allows me to seek opportunities to advance my career.

> 8. **Effectiveness Matters:** *Working smart and excelling in your current role.*
>
> *I have a clear understanding of my accountabilities and I am very effective within my role. I often take on assignments beyond my role for the experience and exposure.*
>
> 9. **Sitting in Front:** *Being recognized in your organization as a rising star.*
>
> *I keep updated on my organization's longer-term goals. I am proactive in promoting myself to leaders and decision makers within my organization.*
>
> 10. **Making Your Mark:** *Leaving your legacy as a leader.*
>
> *I am contributing to the organization, our clients, my teams and my colleagues. I bring a unique skill or perspective that helps our organization be more responsive and effective.*

In my opinion, these ten Career Building Blocks represent the primary factors that will drive a successful career. In today's organizations, there are too many distractions. Internal politics, ineffective colleagues and managers, and an overwhelming number of administrative burdens. My career was built around working directly with clients to find opportunities and build solutions to their environment-related business problems. My biggest challenge was getting my organization to understand the clients' needs so we could develop unique solutions for them. I found myself opting to spend time with our clients rather than getting involved in company politics, hidden agendas, or unnecessary work developed to control the business. I resisted the corner CEO office and remained a road warrior, visiting our teams and our clients. Of course, it is fun to chat it up with colleagues about the newest organizational initiative, changes in corporate policy, or "random crazy idea" your leadership team may pursue. However, create and perpetuate organizational noise at your own risk. Generally, organizational noise only distracts from your ability to execute on your assignment and consumes time otherwise available to focus on your Career Building Blocks.

There are a lot of challenges in developing your career. Some threats come from within the organization, some from the market or industry. Being proactive with your career will help you create opportunities to grow and adjust to changing conditions. Reassessing or changing your career path is encouraged. There are many ways to construct a career. You can help yourself by owning your career and focus your energies on what matters.

Be your best at work by focusing on your effectiveness.

CARREER BUILDING BLOCK	DESCRIPTION	RATING	COMMENTS
CAREER ASPIRATION	I HAVE DEVELOP...	3	A MORNING ROUTINE
ADVISORY TEAM	I HAVE ASSEMBLED...	1	SELECT MENTOR
INVEST IN YOURSELF	I HAVE ROUTINELY LOOKED...	2	TEST FOR PE

Life Care

Life changes fast, keep your priorities clear.

The Life Building Blocks were developed through working with my mentees and conducting interviews with several of my colleagues. The resounding messages I heard were, "I wish I had more time with my friends and family" and, "How can I make more time for myself to do the things I enjoy?" It is difficult to protect the time needed to commit to those things outside of work. Life Building Blocks have been designed to help clarify the most important priorities you may have outside of work.

A primary factor in building your life is to figure out how you can carve out enough time for your career and your life. I encourage you to use Life Building Blocks to narrow down the list of "need to do" activities and focus on a few areas that need the most attention. Trying to do it all can lead to failure and frustration.

10 Life Building Blocks

1. **_Physical Well-Being:_** *Taking care of your health.*

   I have developed a daily routine that protects time for me and allows me to exercise, work out, or otherwise get the physical activity I need.

2. **_Mental Well-Being:_** *Being sharp and focused on your life.*

   I have developed routine activities that allow me to spend time reflecting on my emotional needs and I am engaged in positive activities that benefit my mental health.

3. **_Friends:_** *Maintaining a healthy & diverse network of friends.*

   I routinely engage with a close network of friends who support me and are a positive influence in my career & life. My friendships are diverse and very meaningful to me.

4. **_Family:_** *Healthy engagement with family.*

   I understand my role within my family, and I routinely support my family. I commit the time necessary to fulfill my familial responsibilities.

5. **_Colleagues:_** *Having positive relationships with work peers.*

   I actively identify and connect with work colleagues both in work and outside of work. I enjoy working with my colleagues and they are a strong reason I like my work.

6. **_Spirituality:_** *Seeking out spiritual connection.*

   I am actively involved in my spiritual development. I routinely find time to spend in meditation, at worship, or pursuing other activities that keep me spiritually fulfilled.

7. **_Community:_** *Helping others in need.*

   I participate in community volunteering or leadership roles that are aligned with my passions and that help those in need.

8. **_Self-Care:_** *Taking "me time".*

   I routinely find ways to improve my life through active involvement in hobbies, reading, and connection with self. I regularly treat myself to activities that honor me.

9. **_Continuous Learning:_** *Proactively looking for opportunities to grow.*

> *I set annual goals for continuous learnings and education, both within and outside my career requirements.*
>
> **10. <u>Financial Flexibility:</u>** *Creating a long-term foundation of financial stability.*
>
> *I am on the right track to achieve my financial goals. I routinely evaluate my wealth creation goals and spend time managing investments in my future financial freedom.*

I believe that these ten Life Building Blocks represent the primary factors that will drive a fulfilling life. These building blocks have been developed only to guide you in determining your career-life partnering path. It may be that some of these building blocks do not resonate with you or you do not have the time to pursue them. Use them to your advantage to guide you on what is ultimately important to you.

As with your career, your personal life will bring its own challenges. And your life changes will likely outpace your career changes. Where you live, your partner, your friends, your family, and your financial flexibility will all change over time. Remaining flexible with your life path is advantageous, and paying attention to your life building blocks can help you navigate your life. Things don't always turn out as you plan. Being clear about your priorities will guide you through times of uncertainty. As with your career, there are many ways to construct your life. Be deliberate, and pay attention to what is most important to you.

LIFE BUILDING BLOCK	DESCRIPTION	RATING	COMMENTS
PHYSICAL WELL BEING	I ROUTINELY ...	1	ANNUAL PHYSICAL
MENTAL WELL BEING	I ENGAGE IN ...	5	A GREAT ADVENTURE
FRIENDS	I MAINTAIN A ...	3	EXPAND FRIENDSHIPS

Define life on your terms.

Opportunities & Challenges

Choose to be motivated by your opportunities and challenges.

Let me tell you a story about a time when I felt I was not meeting my commitments to myself, my family, or my career. I had been the CEO of an environmental consulting firm for a couple years and was feeling the pressure, not only from my role at work, but also a dad, a husband, a son, and a brother. I was not happy. My closest family members thought I was a "workaholic." They felt that I had given up on the things that were truly important. But our firm was doing well, we were growing, and I was leading the development of our largest client. It took me a long time to realize I had left my family commitments behind and was not paying attention to them as I truly wanted.

I met with my family and my spouse to discuss the mess I had gotten myself into. During our discussions, I recognized it was not easy to fulfill all my expectations for my family and my career. There was no choice but to reprioritize my world of career and life. I wish I had recognized the path I was on earlier; it would have been much easier to make the necessary changes.

Now that you have completed the Career-Life Care Assessment, you are able to clearly recognize the opportunities and challenges that you face in developing your career-life partnership. Your opportunities are those building blocks you rated yourself the highest (5). Your challenges are those building blocks you rated yourself the lowest (1). Write these down; you will use these building blocks later as you develop your Career-Life Partnering Plan.

I want to share with you some examples of opportunities and challenges that have been shared with me through my individual and group mentoring work. Developing your opportunities and challenges should be relatively straightforward after the work you have just done. Put your own words to them, highlight key messages to yourself, and frame your necessary actions. Use your notes as part of your Career-Life Partnering Plan, share them with your organization, or keep them to yourself. You have already done a lot of work by identifying those areas that will continue to drive you towards career life partnering.

Your career opportunities could include:

- ***Career Aspiration:*** *I am clear on my long-term career goals and I am on the right track. I will continue to review my career aspirations on an annual basis and make necessary changes.*

- ***Networking Matters:*** *Recently, I have gotten involved in industry groups and feel good about my relationships with my colleagues and industry peers. I plan to take on more of a leadership role in industry conferences and organizations.*

- ***Effectiveness Matters:*** *I understand my primary assignments and am executing on them well. I plan on seeking additional assignments to stretch into new areas and grow my exposure to the organization.*

Your career challenges could include:

- ***Advisory Team:*** *I have informal relationships with people who support me, but I am missing a few key members of my advisory team. I will formalize a mentoring relationship and seek an advisor to help me with financial planning.*

- ***Investing in Yourself:*** *I have not advanced my education or professional credits. I need to commit to completing my certification and finalizing my professional training requirements.*

- ***Sitting in Front:*** *I work well with my manager, but I have not taken the time to expand my relationships with other leaders in the organization. I will make it a point to introduce myself to company leaders throughout the organization.*

Often, we focus on the challenges facing us. Be sure to also leverage the opportunities you have created. Many of our opportunities are recognized by others in the organization; continuing to develop these opportunities will lead to more success. Don't take the opportunities you have created for granted. Work on your challenges while leveraging your opportunities.

Your life opportunities could include:

- ***Friends:*** *I have a diverse network of friends who support me outside of work. I value these friendships and will continue to develop them.*

- ***Colleagues:*** *I enjoy my work colleagues. I respect them and they respect me. We do everything we can to make work exciting and fun. We can rely on each other to lend a helping hand when necessary.*

- ***Self-Care:*** *I protect my "me time." I am a history buff and enjoy reading novels about the archaeology of the world. I am committed to finishing my reading on the lost cities of the Incas.*

Your life challenges could include:

- ***Physical Well-Being:*** *I get routine physicals but I missed my last one. I need to commit to a routine regiment of health care, including checkups and weekly exercise.*

- ***Family:*** *I maintain a good relationship with my partner, but I need to spend more time celebrating our life together.*

- **Community:** *I live in a great community, and I would like to get involved in an organization that supports community engagement in education, health care, or the environment.*

	OPPORTUNITY	CHALLENGES
CAREER	- PROFESSIONAL BRAND - NETWORKING MATTERS - -	- ADVISORY TEAM - CAREER ASPIRATION - -
LIFE	- COMMUNITY - SPIRITUAL - -	- WELL BEING - FINANCIAL FLEXIBILITY - -

As you see, these building blocks are simple and address some very important parts to having a successful career and life. Your opportunities and challenges will change over time as you accept more responsibilities in your career and your life. What if you are offered a promotion that requires a relocation? Can you survive a period of unemployment? How will you manage an addition to your family?

There is no magic here. I hope the Career Life-Care Assessment gives you a way to identify those simple things you can do to relieve any frustration you may have in your career-life partnership. Sometimes the most helpful things are the simplest. Stay ahead of your needs. It is always easier to change course along the way rather than waiting until you are in a crisis.

Nothing remains the same. Change, in and outside of work will always challenge you to reassess your priorities. I encourage my mentees to use the Career-Life Care Assessment annually and make the needed adjustments to your priorities and Career Life Partnering Plan.

Enhance your opportunities and improve on your challenges.

Summary

Making time to assess yourself against a few meaningful career and life priorities is not easy. It is your opportunity to determine if you are on track or where you might prioritize your time moving forward. Your assessment will change over the course of your career and life journey. Check up on yourself and reflect on your accomplishments.

- ✓ *Career Care Assessment: Ten career building blocks that are important to fully developing your career*

- ✓ *Life Care Assessment: Ten life building blocks that can guide you to a fulfilling life*

- ✓ *Opportunities and Challenges: Identify your priorities to leverage or enhance your success*

Your career will pull you in many directions: The challenges of a client, the deadlines to your manager or colleagues, or the overtime hours needed to finish a critical project. I am hopeful that the time you spend with your career will be challenging, exciting, and meaningful. However, remember you also have a life to live. You give a lot to your career. Get something back that allows you to achieve your life goals.

Remember, you have a life to live.

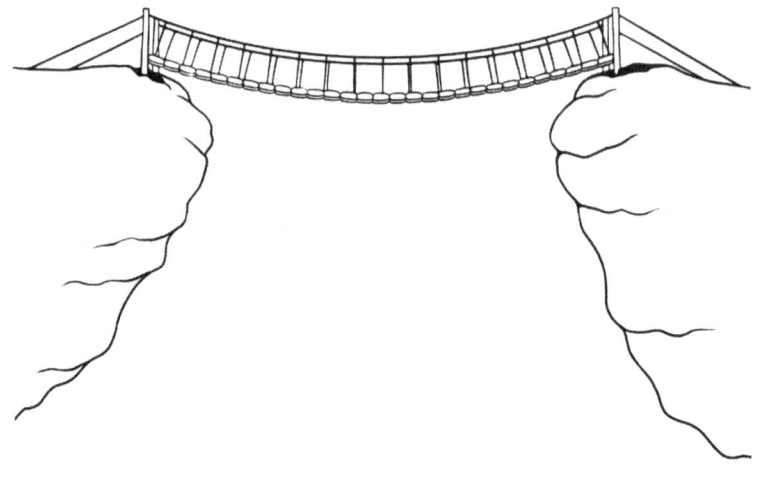

CHAPTER 7

Career-Life Partnering Matrix

"The journey of a thousand miles begins with one step." – Lao Tzu

Your priorities will change with time and that is OK.

You have all heard the terms "live to work" and "work to live." Where are you on your career life journey related to these terms? Where are you spending your time, your energy, and your focus? The Career-Life Partnering Matrix was built to allow you to quickly compare your current commitment to your career and life. This matrix is useful in directionally pointing out to you where you may want to spend more effort, career or life.

Developing a career-life partnership is an ongoing effort. If you are an employee, you need to own both your career and life goals. As an employer, offering options to your employees to develop both their career and life goals will lead to a more sustainable and engaged workforce. In my consulting business, I work with employee-owned, family-owned, and corporate-owned organizations. Private and public institutions that see their employees as integral to the success of their mission can offer a key advantage to the career developer. Those organizations that mistrust or disengage in the development of their employees do not make good partners. While the ownership structure can influence the organizational culture, nothing is more important than the leadership and commitment by the organization to your well-being.

Your ability to construct a partnership with your career will depend significantly on your choice of industry and organization. Regardless of your choice, the Career-Life Partnering Model will provide you with the tools you need to achieve your career and life goals.

So, how do you determine where you are in developing your career-life partnership? Where should your forward efforts be applied? Can you further leverage your opportunities and address your challenges?

The Career-Life Partnering Matrix allows you to validate how you are managing the complexities of both your career and life. Changing how you prioritize your time and commitments may depend on where you are on your career-life partnership journey.

Informed, Enlightened, & Purposeful

If you're stuck, maybe you should reevaluate your career-life priorities.

You have successfully compared your current behaviors and priorities against the twenty Career and Life Building Blocks. You have rated yourself against the ideal behaviors associated with each of the building blocks. Now let's define a few simple categories that might help describe your commitment to achieving those critical behaviors for both your career and life. Based on your total score across all the building blocks, you will find yourself in one of three categories:

- *Informed (0–30):* You are aware of the Career and Life Building Blocks that can help you achieve a career-life partnership. You may be new to your career or reinventing your career. You may have several actions you want to take to address your challenges. Start small, with the key challenges you feel will bring you the greatest value. Not all the Career and Life Building Blocks are created equal! Look for those opportunities and challenges in your career and life that you can take on now. You decide the importance of each building block and pursue your career-life partnership.

- *Enlightened (31–70):* You have begun developing the necessary behaviors in support of achieving your career and life goals. Find ways to reinforce your behaviors to continue your development towards full career-life partnering. Your challenges and opportunities to enhance yourself will change over time; move forward with those that will help you over the next one to three years. You also have experience with what it takes to be successful, so leverage your success for additional progress. Prioritize and address the Career and Life Building Blocks you see appropriate.

- *Purposeful (71–100):* You have achieved the behaviors to reach your career or life goals. Selectively address those Career and Life Building Blocks you see appropriate to sustain your

> desired outcomes. You have accomplished a lot; continue to project both your career and life forward. Challenge your career aspirations and life goals, convince yourself you are on the right track. Your action plan will likely be very specific on where you can help yourself the most. Your positive behaviors are in place. Reinforce your behaviors and address the remaining Career and Life Building Blocks you see as helpful.

These categories have been defined based on your responses to your Career-Life Care Assessment, but they are really a reflection of your mindset toward your career and your life. As you pursue your career and life goals, you will likely find yourself prioritizing your commitments differently from time to time. This is expected and OK. Your commitments, your priorities, and your mindset towards your career and life should remain aligned with your current and future obligations.

Introducing the Career-Life Partnering Matrix

Pursue, achieve, and sustain your career and life goals.

Let's take what we have learned from your Career-Life Care Assessment to shed some light on current and possibly future priorities. The Career-Life Partnering Matrix will give you your current career-life partnering status. Where are you focusing your time and efforts: On your career or your life? You will find yourself in one of nine priority preferences. These priority preferences reflect your mindset of where you currently prioritize your career and life.

LIFE PURPOSEFUL	WORK TO LIVE	PRIORITIZE YOUR CAREER	CAREER LIFE PARTNERING
LIFE ENLIGHTENED	LIFE OR CAREER	CONTINUE YOUR PARTNERING JOURNEY	PRIORITIZE YOUR LIFE
LIFE INFORMED	BEGIN YOUR PARTNERING JOURNEY	CAREER OR LIFE	LIVE TO WORK
	CAREER INFORMED	CAREER ENLIGHTENED	CAREER PURPOSEFUL

The priority preferences include the following:

- ◎ ***Beginning Your Partnering Journey:*** *As a new career developer, maybe in your Acquire or Develop career lifecycle stage, you could be just entering the workforce and developing a clear view on your career and life goals. This is absolutely OK! You have already started to identify the important building blocks in both your career and life. Give yourself time to explore career options and establish your life priorities.*

- ***Life or Career:*** *As you assess your current priorities, maybe you should consider asking yourself more questions about how you will achieve your career aspiration. Will you be pleased with the outcome of your career if you remain on the same path forward? You have identified your career building blocks that need attention. Put in the work to challenge your view of your career.*

- ***Career or Life:*** *Your current priorities are focused on developing your career. It may be time to reflect on your life goals and commit to enhancing your life building blocks. Will your current path allow you to achieve your life goals? Here is where you challenge yourself to give more effort in achieving your life goals.*

- ***Work to Live:*** *You may consider your commitments outside of your career more important than those within it. Maybe your career aspiration is taking a back seat to your pursuit of a healthy and happy life. You have chosen to put your life goals ahead of your career goals. Is your current path sustainable and will it provide you the freedom to continue your life's journey? Spending more time on your career building blocks could lead to a more satisfying career and life partnership.*

- ***Live to Work:*** *Working hard and setting your career goals ahead of your life goals may be necessary at times. However, if you maintain a live-to-work mindset throughout your career journey, you are likely to miss out on a lot of life. Is your current path forward sustainable and allow you to reach your life goals? Spending more time on your life building blocks could lead to a more satisfying life and career partnership.*

- **Prioritize Your Career:** You have an opportunity to achieve a meaningful career-life partnership. You have developed the behaviors required to promote and advance your life and career goals. You have recognized the benefits of a healthy and happy life. Maintaining commitments to your life building blocks and further developing your career building blocks will move you to a career-life partnership.

- **Prioritize Your Life:** You have an opportunity to achieve a meaningful career-life partnership. You have developed the behaviors required to promote and advance your career and life goals. You have recognized the benefits of your career. Maintaining commitments to your career building blocks and further developing your life building blocks will move you to a career-life partnership.

- **Continue Your Partnering Journey:** You have been able to commit to both your career and your life priorities. You are addressing those important building blocks of both a successful career and a meaningful life. Continue your journey and keep those career and life goals ahead of you.

- **Career-Life Partnering:** Congratulations! You are in position to partner with your career and have the life you want and deserve. It is hard to develop the discipline to establish a career-life partnership and even harder to maintain the priorities and behaviors that got you to this relationship between your career and life. It was tough getting here, acknowledge that. Also know that it is even tougher maintaining these behaviors!

Your priorities will change over time, as your career and life change. As I reflect on my career and life, I have visited each one of these priority positions at one time or another. There is nothing wrong with any of these priority positions, for they each can provide you with a perspective on where you are today and maybe what to prioritize moving forward. If you look to change your mindset and more actively drive your career or your life, you have the building blocks to clarify those necessary activities.

Your mindset drives your priorities.

Summary

Moving towards and staying in a career-life partnership will be a lifetime journey. I even find myself, well into my Transition career lifecycle phase, challenging myself to weigh both my career and life goals. Where do I choose to spend my time? Can I do everything in life that I have wanted to do, or do I need to manage my expectations? It is never good to leave too many questions at the end of your career or life, so challenge yourself with the right questions now, while you have time to pursue your opportunities.

- ✔ ***Remain informed, enlightened, and purposeful:** Your mindset on balancing your career and life will directly affect your success. Uncover those critical elements of both your career and life that might help you create a career life partnership.*

- ✔ ***Use the Career-Life Partnership Matrix:** Developing your career-life partnership is a journey. Find where you are on your journey and work on those elements that will help you move forward.*

Besides commitment, your second most powerful asset is your time. How you choose to use your time will likely determine the success of both your career and your life. Sometimes it is hard to see a path to a more fulfilling career or happier life. I want to assure you that you will be successful if you remain committed to using your time focused on what matters in building a meaningful career and a great life.

Live to work or work to live? Maybe, find something in between.

CHAPTER 8

Essential Partnering Elements

"Alone we can do so little; together we can do so much" – Helen Keller

Partnering Ain't Easy
Now it's time to get more into this idea of truly partnering with your career. Let's explore. Throughout this book I have avoided using the term "work-life balance", instead I have used "career-life partnering." The simplest way for me to think about the difference, is that your career and your life are two of the most important things you will develop over your years of breathing and doing. Both your career and your life require attention and need to be managed throughout your lifetime. This dance between career and life is long term, sometimes messy, and requires a lot of work to achieve a successful career and happy life.

Occasionally, we will come out of *balance,* but if we have the right *partnership,* we will adjust and realign our priorities. Taking the long view of both your career and life can bring some reassurance that you have time to develop both. I have missed several anniversaries, birthdays and many of my children's sporting events while I was building my career. We were also able to travel together as a family and experience what the world has to offer. We have created many memories as a family, and I am happy to have had this time together. These days, anniversaries and birthdays have more meaning!

I believe there are some real and obvious challenges in moving your career life partnership forward. Many of you will be independent of any organization or company. You could be very happy working on your own and fortunate enough to make a living doing just that. Others of you reading this book will be working in an organization, a company, an institution, or group. Let me call them organizations. These organizations construct cultures and management structures and hire employees to deliver a service or product to their markets or clients. Of course there are numerous industries to choose from: technology to healthcare, engineering to manufacturing. Our global economies are producing tremendous opportunities for organizations and their employees.

Your next step will be to build your Career-Life Partnering Plan. Before you do, let me share with you my experiences in building a career-life partnership. As with any partnership, it is not easy, and you will be met with many challenges. Stay focused and have confidence in your abilities to succeed. A good partner will also get you unstuck occasionally, but you can't rely on them to make your decisions based on your priorities.

We will come out of balance, but if we have the right partner, we will adjust and realign our priorities.

Building a partnership with your career requires patience. You may already be in a career and an organization that you believe will be a good partner. If you are not positioned to partner with your career, reach out to your mentors, coaches, family, or friends. Get the support you need to pursue your career-life partnership.

Partnerships are developed over time. They evolve, they succeed, and they fail. Whether you are a new career developer or have been at it for a while, you may recognize the art in developing partnerships. The following eight essential partnering elements might help you navigate your partner relationship.

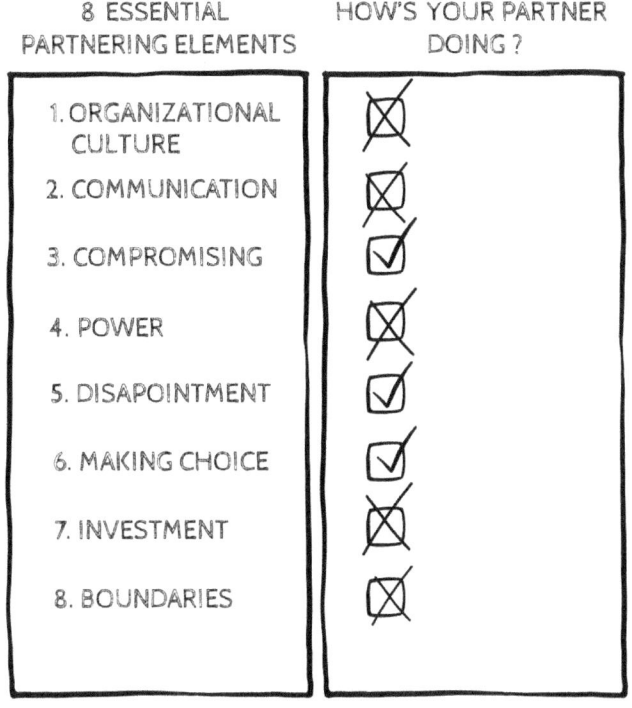

Organizational Culture

You are one partner; your career is the other. Assuming you can trust yourself to define your goals and make good decisions, your career will be available primarily based on your organization's response to your desired outcomes. Can you trust your partner?

Organizations often have development planning processes, helping you build your career within the organization. Rarely do organizations look towards helping you with your life. That's up to you. Obviously, there are some legitimate boundaries organizations have with their employees to protect themselves and you. I find that the best organizations have developed learning cultures and are secure enough in their businesses to help their employees in their careers and life. Enlightened organizations and good managers will be concerned with you successfully achieving your life goals as well as your professional goals.

I have had a mentoring assignment from a company for two years. The leaders of the organization have asked me to mentor new employees who are entering a new industry and a new professional role. My mentoring relationship with one of the employees started with basic "coaching" focused on his immediate effectiveness, knowledge of the industry, and client-relationship development skills. His life had changed, and he was looking for more flexibility in a less-demanding environment and he wanted to get back to a familiar industry. While maintaining confidentiality and professional dialogue, my mentee approached his manager to discuss. He has now moved on to a new role outside the organization.

The loss of an employee from an organization can be very costly and disruptive. However, this organization understands that their team must be committed to the organization and their individual assignments. Everyone needs to work at their optimal levels, and they only do that if they value their role, and they can achieve a career-life partnership!

Can you trust your organization as a partner?

Communication

Organizational culture sets the stage for an effective career-life partnership, and individual managers must be approachable and accept the role of partner advocate. Organizations typically structure their work teams under a manager. Managers tend to have work teams from eight to ten, though of course this differs from organization to organization. If you look at an organization of one hundred, there are ten to twelve managers overseeing other employees. In an organization of one thousand people, there are one hundred to one hundred and twenty-five managers. And so on!

What are the odds that you will land with the right manager for you? If you have the right manager, you know by now; if you do not, you will also know by now. Your manager should be your partner advocate. Realistically, many managers are underequipped to address career and life coaching. In some cases, managers can be selfish, not wanting to lose a top performer to a new opportunity or a life ambition.

The best managers will ask a lot of questions when it comes to your career aspirations and life goals. If they do not ask, they are not interested or don't understand one of their primary assignments: employee effectiveness. Be prepared to be clear on what you expect from your organization and your manager.

One morning over a cup of coffee, as we were preparing for a client presentation, I asked one of my team members if he would be interested in an assignment in Germany. I explained the organizational and client needs, and he seemed somewhat interested. The role had not been formally developed and depended on a significant client award, meaning there were a lot of unknowns at the time. Over the next few weeks, he spoke with his spouse and three children and he confirmed his interest to me. I don't think we did anything special that morning; I only asked a simple question. But the impact was significant. He spent three years in Germany and came back with a new energy and focus on his career and life.

Your manager should be your partner advocate.

Compromising

Expecting your partner to take on all the risks or conform to your interests is not realistic. However, your career and life journey should provide you incremental benefits along the way. Your priorities may or may not be aligned with those of your partner organization. Many times, partnerships fail because there are no shared goals between the partners. And even if priorities are aligned, the urgency each party feels in accomplishing them may differ.

It is important to remember that your partner organization has many priorities, including addressing the unique priorities of many employees, not just yours. Your organization has to choose how they will address the needs of individual employees and the collective group of employees within the organization. Think about it this way: If you want to take a three-month trek in the Himalayans for a once-in-a-lifetime adventure, do all your colleagues get three months away from work, too? Who will manage your workload in your absence? Imagine the complexity of managing a fully partnered workforce! Be respectful and try to understand how your expectations will affect the organization. Consider remote working. Many employees prefer this to the traditional office model and are quite productive in it. Remote working models also have unique challenges around communication, building a consistent company culture, and the technological investments required to maintain connectivity and security. Your partner organization has to manage expectations around those, too.

My career was working with oil and gas clients, managing relationships with several global energy companies. These companies have U.S. headquarters in Houston, so that's where I spent a lot of my time visiting and promoting business. The challenge for me was that my wife and her career, and my children, lived in the Midwest, outside of Minneapolis. The grand compromise for me and my career was to be able to work remotely my entire career. My partner organizations were understanding and allowed me this opportunity to build a career and live a life where my family desired to be. I am forever grateful for this.

The compromises were clear. My partner organizations funded my travel, lodging, and meals. They understood that I would not always be available for client meetings or industry events. And I understood that I would not have a traditional work structure. I generally worked very long hours, missed many family events, and had a hard time developing friendships outside of my work colleagues. Was I in balance? Likely no! However, I feel I had a great career and an opportunity to build a great life.

Are your priorities aligned with your partner?

Power

Could you walk away from your job right now? For many, the answer is no. True partners need each other to be successful. Determining where the power is in a relationship can be helpful in understanding the value each partner brings to the partnership. In a career, the power equation is generally built around the employee earning compensation for delivering desired organizational results. Your ability to deliver results to your organization will assist you in your partnership discussions.

One of the first concepts of my mentoring is the idea of role effectiveness. This is the minimum requirement for developing a long-lasting career-life partnership. Effectiveness in your role starts with a clear understanding of your assignment, the resources available to you, and how your success will be measured. Once these elements are clear, then it is up to the employee to achieve and produce. The unfortunate reality is that organizations spend more time with underperformers than those who are performing well and would benefit from a true partnership. High performers may have to take extra effort to engage with their organization to develop their careers. Take action and be realistic in your expectations. Your requirements of your partner and your career should allow you to have a meaningful career and fulfilled life.

I have had numerous colleagues during my career who have been very effective in their roles. They have worked hard to build their knowledge, relationships, and work habits to help them excel in their careers. Many of these colleagues have moved on to new, more challenging roles outside their original organizations. Not always, but many times, the good people in an organization leave first. Recently, a colleague of mine who is a senior leader accepted a new role with a previous competitor. She liked her previous organization, but they were unable to fulfill her needs for her career-life journey. From the outside looking in, I did not see any difference in the organizations. However, after speaking with her, I found she trusts the new organization and her new manager more to help her achieve her goals. She found a new partner!

As for my own career, I have been employed in two industries and five organizations and have had more than thirty roles. My point is that your current role is the least important factor in developing a career-life partnership. Roles are temporary, and your ability to position yourself for change is critical to achieving your career aspirations and life goals. Demonstrate your value and make the ask!

Your effectiveness gives you the opportunity to make the ask!

Disappointment

No one likes to fail, to feel disappointment when things do not turn out the way we envisioned, planned for, or desired. Many organizations are risk adverse and not open to trying new things, while others are constantly experimenting with their services and products to better serve their markets or clients. Consider how fear of failure or disappointment might play into how "risk willing" a company is. Partners accept and share the risks of achieving mutual goals. Nimble organizations are those who can build, deploy, and reconstruct themselves easily and routinely. Other organizations are slower to react but remain predictable. What type of partner are you looking for?

Setting realistic goals is the best first step in avoiding disappointment with your partner organization. In order to move your career and life forward, you will need to push yourself. Try things you have never done, go places you have never visited, and make decisions you have never faced before. You are doing these things now, on an ongoing basis, and it is how you are navigating your career and life today. Accepting failure in yourself and your partner will help you remain focused on success. Sounds weird, right? It's true! Push through feelings of disappointment, for if you focus only on the failures, there will be no time or energy left to focus on constructing future successes. Living your life without holding on to disappointments may be your truest measure of a life well lived.

One of my mentees decided it was time for him to start his own business. He left the firm and ventured out on his own to start a competing company. As you can imagine, the separation was not pleasant and there were hard feelings from both parties. Now twenty years later, I recently interviewed him for this book. I asked him why he left. "I had to," he said. "I had to prove to myself I could start and lead my own business. I regret the way I left, but I don't regret leaving." His business ended up failing after a few years, but he learned a lot about himself, his capabilities, and his passions in life. I admire him for taking the risk, trusting his instincts, and reinventing his career and life based on his experience.

Living your life without any regrets may be your truest measure of a life well lived.

Making Choices

Saying yes is easy; saying no is hard! I don't believe you can do everything well, and you definitely cannot do everything well simultaneously. The best way to fail is to try to do too much. There will be many opportunities for you to explore both your career and life ambitions. In the simplest form, life is about creating opportunities! It is up to you to sort through those opportunities you feel provide you the best scenery along your career and life journey.

The fear of missing out (FOMO) is a real thing. I still live with a feeling that I could be doing more, traveling more, making more money . . . you name it. I am always wondering what's next. Do I grow my consulting business? Do I write another book? Do I really retire and call it good enough? What I have learned is that if you are always thinking about the future and your desires for more, you miss out on the present. Enjoying today while preparing for the future are keys to developing your career-life success.

I admire my wife, Katie, for many reasons and mostly her ability to live in the moment and say yes to those things that have been important in our lives. Katie developed a career over many years working with children, helping them become successful. She was able to seamlessly integrate her roles as a teacher, mother, friend, and spouse. Every step along the way, she said no to things that did not bring value and yes to only those things that supported our life goals. Without her, I would not have been able to have the career or life I have had!

Having choices is the simplest form of having achieved success. Your choices will determine whether you remain successful in the future.

Saying yes is easy; saying no is hard!

Investment Needs

We show our commitments by the investments we make in our partnerships. Without proper investments, partnerships fail. Even with the best intentions, if the right people are not engaged or if time is not protected to build the partnership, it will fail. Your commitment must come first. You must ensure that you are committing the time and money to move your career-life partnership forward.

I generally start a relationship with a new mentee by meeting every other week. After about six months, we switch to monthly calls or meetings. In each meeting, my mentee will bring a few topics to discuss. This is not a lot of time, but it is the only direct mentoring time we have to discuss challenges and construct strategies to support a career-life partnership. I also encourage monthly updates with their manager, as I feel strongly that my mentees should have an advisory team. This advisory team could include friends and family, a financial advisor, an attorney, a therapist, and a health professional. Are you committed to making this investment?

One of my mentees is extremely busy at work, but she has identified both a career gap and a life need. She has a goal of becoming a professional engineer, requiring a rigorous professional exam. In addition, she has identified the desire to evaluate and construct a sustainable financial portfolio of investments for her and her family. Obviously, these are important steps forward in creating a successful career-life partnership.

As you use the Career-Life Partnering Model, you will identify your opportunities and challenges. Are you prepared to make the necessary commitments and investments? Of course, you should be able to depend on your partner organization to invest in you, but the motivation and urgency will need to come from you. I think you will, but it will take continued investment of your time and money to be successful.

Having a supportive advisory team is important.

Boundaries

Partnerships need boundaries. Likely one of the biggest challenges you will face in developing a career-life partnership with your organization will be to understand each other's boundaries. In today's world, organizations have many legal and ethical boundaries placed on them to protect themselves and their work teams, including those around confidentiality, uniform salary and benefit administration, financial disclosures, and several others that are both needed and necessary.

The natural tendency of your partner organizations likely will be to resist helping you outside of work. Their primary obligation to you, as an employee, is to treat you fairly and provide you the support you need to achieve their goals as outlined for the assignment or position. That's OK, but I don't think this alone is sufficient to motivate, retain, and engage the best employees. So, given this natural bias, much of your attention should be focused on designing a dialogue with your partner organization, manager, and mentor that will keep them informed on your career and life goals. The context you provide during these discussions will assist them in making decisions about your work assignments, future roles, and development needs.

I am currently engaged in an assignment where two senior leaders of a client company have expressed their desire to do more. They are both successful and performing members of the company leadership team and each feels they can bring greater value to the firm in a different role. One of the leaders sees a move for their family and another leader desires more time working with clients and business development. Both aspirations are aligned with the organization and will bring value to both the employees and the organization.

The challenge is that in order to reach these aspirations, there will need to be changes in both their professional and life paths. As an organization, what can you do? As an employee, what are you willing to do? Given the culture and leadership at this organization, it is more likely than not that a solution will emerge. Whatever the solution, it will require modifications in the relationships the employees have with the organization. This change will take time and will only be possible through partnership.

Successful partnerships have boundaries.

Summary

So, you are now positioned to build your career-life partnership! This is great and you are very lucky and now you can move full steam ahead. As you move forward, you will likely develop multiple partnerships with numerous organizations and managers. Your roles will change, and you will need to navigate new partners and colleagues. As you are negotiating your partnerships, stay focused and remember the essential partnering elements:

- ✓ *Organizational Culture: Enlightened organizations and good managers will be concerned with you successfully achieving your life goals as well as your professional goals.*

- ✓ *Communication: The best managers will ask a lot of questions when it comes to your career aspirations and life goals.*

- ✓ *Compromising: Many times, partnerships fail due to the inability of the partners to share common goals. Align your priorities and urgency to accomplish your goals.*

- ✓ *Power: Your role effectiveness is the minimum requirement for developing a long-lasting career-life partnership.*

- ✓ *Disappointment: There will be disappointments and failures along your journey. Push through disappointment to the other side, where you can turn what you have learned into tools for future success.*

- ✔ ***Making Choices:*** *It is up to you to identify and pursue those opportunities you feel provide the best scenery along your career and life journey.*

- ✔ ***Investment Needs:*** *Even with the best intentions, if the right people are not engaged or if time is not protected to build the partnership, it will fail. Invest in yourself and find others who will invest in you.*

- ✔ ***Boundaries:*** *The natural tendency for your partner organizations will be to resist helping you outside of work. Focus on designing a dialogue with your partner organization, your manager, and your mentor, that will inform them of your career and life goals.*

Your career-life partnering journey will bring you opportunities to engage with, learn from, and establish friendships with colleagues, managers, and mentors. Start building those relationships now!

Partner with those who support your goals and your urgency.

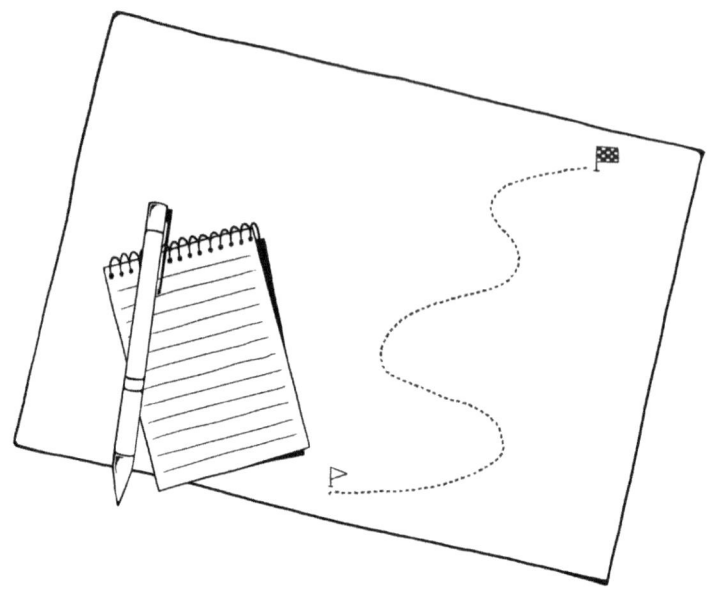

CHAPTER 9

Career Life Partnering Plan

"Action expresses priorities" – Mahatma Ghandhi

You can't plan for everything, but why not plan for those things you can? Once you begin your career, you will likely have fifty or more years of career and life ahead of you. Every year of your career-life journey will be different. Sometimes your challenges and opportunities can be controlled and sometimes they cannot. I have always thought of a plan as a way to point you in the right direction. A good plan can alert you when you are veering off course and to remind you of your destination and the path you have chosen. Plans should be meaningful to you; if they are not, then you will not see them as important.

How many to-do lists have you made for yourself? Making a to-do list is making a plan! Put hard things and easy things on your to-do list. I do. The hard things may take a little time, but the easy things will get crossed off quickly. Of course, the harder items on your to do list are likely the most critical, but doing some of your easier tasks can motivate you to do more! You have done a lot of work to this point: You completed your Career-Life Care Assessment, you identified your opportunities and challenges, and you positioned yourself on the Career-Life Partnering Matrix. You know what needs to be done, so now let's build your Career-Life Partnering Plan to help you take action.

Some considerations when developing your plan:

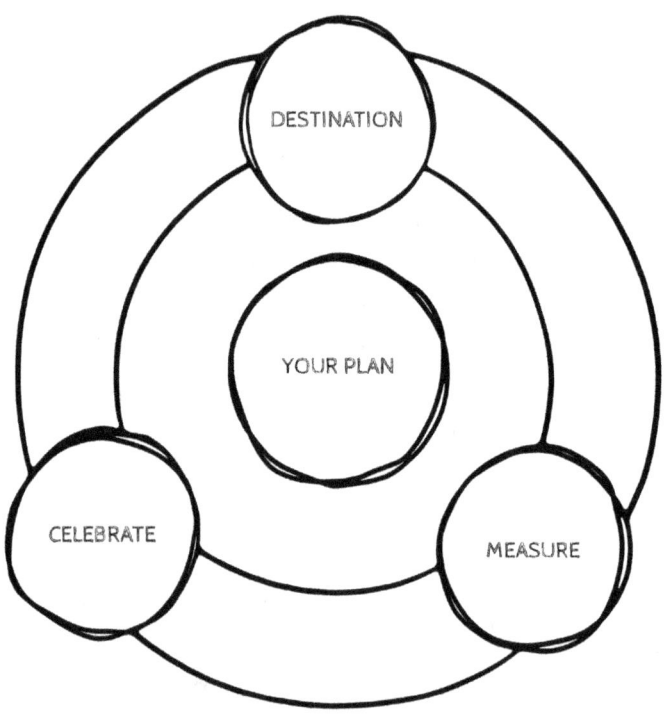

> ◎ **Set a destination you believe in.** Your career and life aspirations should be aligned with your passion and unique to you. When your journey gets difficult, you will want to know your destination is worth the fight. This part of your plan might be

the most difficult to create. It is easy to describe where you are today, it is much harder to project yourself into the future. Set aside some time to dream, to talk with your mentors, friends, and family. Remember, you don't need to be perfect. And sometimes you may think your aspirations are not achievable, but do not limit yourself!

- **Reach for the sky but keep your feet planted on the ground.** A favorite client of mine gave me this advice many years ago. Expect to accomplish big things but set tangible and achievable goals along the way. Achieving your goals is a great way to motivate you to do more. Inspect your goals and your ability to accomplish them regularly. Seek input from others, but don't let them measure your success. You will be the only one who really knows if you are on the right path to accomplishing your goals.

- **Celebrate your success.** As you achieve your milestones along your career-life journey, be sure to celebrate your success with those who have helped you. One of the greatest joys you will have will be to recognize your accomplishments and share your success with others. Lastly, don't keep your plan quiet. Share it with your advisory team and your manager and include it in your professional/personal development plan with your organization.

Let's Put It All Together!

We started many pages ago talking about the Career-Life Partnering Model. We have described the components of the model and have dug in with some detail on its purpose and use. This last component of the model is the Career-Life Partnering Plan.

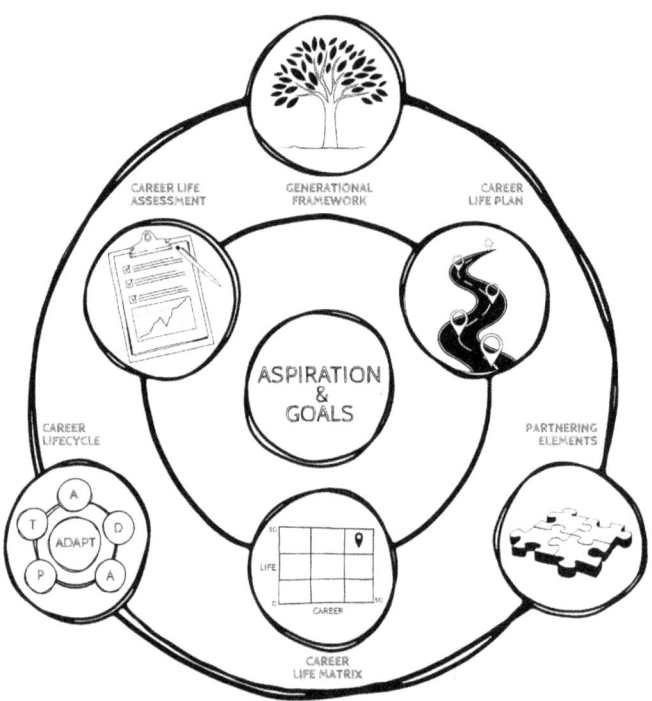

It's time to build your plan! I suggest you take seven steps to realize your action plan. For each step, I have posed a few key questions and provided examples on how you might frame your responses. Of course, this is your plan, so use the words and level of detail you see necessary to guide you.

STEP 1. Aspirations

Do you have your career and life aspirations? What are they? Have you written them down yet? How often do you review them? Have you shared your aspirations with your partners?

> **Example:** I will have a career that is rewarding, builds relationships, and provides me financial flexibility to retire at age sixty. I will develop a career that supports my needs related to travel, exploration, my family, and my friends.

STEP 2. ADAPT Lifecycle

What career lifecycle stage are you in now? What is your next career lifecycle stage? What do you need to do to prepare yourself for the next career lifecycle stage? Does your organization provide you the opportunity to move forward?

> **Example:** I am in the Acquire career lifecycle stage. My next stage is Develop. I need to prepare myself for a job, learn how to be in the workforce, and further refine my career aspirations.

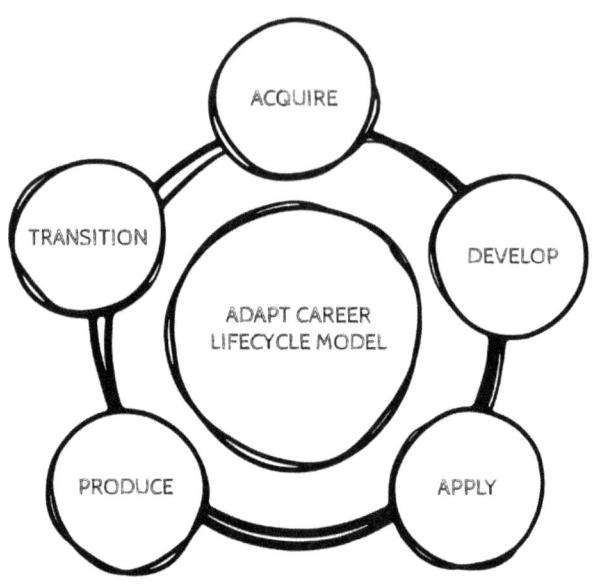

STEP 3. Career and Life Building Blocks

What have you identified as your top opportunities and challenges from your Career-Life Care Assessment? What specifically will you do to leverage your opportunities and address your challenges?

> **Example:** *Career Challenge - Advisory Team.* I will develop a relationship with both an internal and external mentor by the end of the year. *Life Opportunity - Family.* I will

continue to protect the time I spend with my family. We will make time this year for a family holiday.

	OPPORTUNITY	CHALLENGES
CAREER	- PROFESSIONAL BRAND - NETWORKING MATTERS -	- ADVISORY TEAM - CAREER ASPIRATION -
LIFE	- COMMUNITY - SPIRITUAL -	- WELL BEING - FINANCIAL FLEXIBILITY -

STEP 4. Three- and Five-Year Career Goals

What specific roles do you believe are best to move your career forward in three years? In five years? Are these roles available in your current organization?

Example: *Three-Year Role - Senior Engineer.* I will seek a role that allows me to expand my technical background and execute larger projects. *Five-Year Role - Account Manager.* I will become an account manager in five years. I will leverage my technical skills to build business relationships with key clients.

STEP 5. Three- and Five -Year Life Goals

What are the specific goals you believe are consistent with your desired life? What can you do to explore your passion and build your relationships outside of work in three years? In five years?

> **Example:** *Three-Year Goals:* Buy a house/condo and pay off my student loans. *Five-Year Goals:* Relocate closer to family, take a long adventure, and have $100,000 in my retirement account.

STEP 6. Career and Life Gaps

What actions/gaps do you need to take to achieve your role and goal expectations? What personal or professional improvements do you need to make to achieve your longer-term goals in three years? In five years?

> **Example:** *Three-Year Career Goal:* Get my Professional Registration. *Five-Year Career Goal:* Get my MBA and get a new client. *Three-Year Life Goal:* Save for my house down payment. *Five-Year Goal:* Maximize my retirement contributions.

STEP 7. Career-Life Roadmap

Let's put your plan on a map. Continue on your career-life partner journey!

Example: Career-Life Roadmap

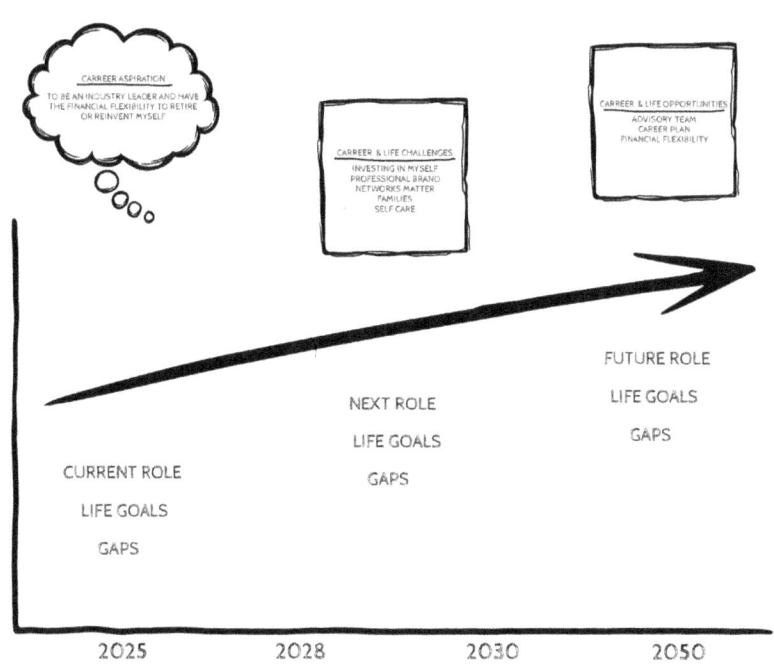

Summary

Plans are a funny thing! Some people love building plans, others don't. For me, they are a must. Generally, my plans are very high level and do not have a lot of detail. I find that I get too uptight if I do not have a plan, and I also get uptight if my plan is too rigid. I urge you to develop a plan, one that is compatible with the way you work. Maybe it is a checklist on your refrigerator, or maybe it is on your daily calendar as reminders. Your plan should include the following:

- ✓ *Aspirations: Set your longer-term vision for your career and life.*

- ✓ *ADAPT Career Lifecycle Model: Use this model to find where you are today and what will be your next career lifecycle stage.*

- ✓ *Career and Life Building Blocks: Identify your opportunities and challenges and prepare yourself to take action on them.*

- ✓ *Three- and Five-Year Career Goals: Be specific and try to visualize your next career steps.*

- ✓ *Three- and Five-Year Life Goals: Be specific on how you will move forward with your life goals.*

- ✓ *Career and Life Gaps: Identify those personal or professional improvements you can make to advance your career-life partnership.*

- ✓ *Career and Life Roadmap: Consolidate your actions into a simple map to illustrate your overall plan.*

Have fun in developing your plan. Encourage your mentor, coach, or friends/family to help you construct your plan. Use your plan in support of any professional development planning that your organization may administer. Challenge yourself, reach for the stars as you create a compelling and inspiring plan. Hold yourself to your highest standards and seek out adventure, experiences, and opportunities that give you joy and fulfillment. Your plan should work for you, Make it yours!

"If you don't know where you are going, you'll end up someplace else." – Yogi Berra

CHAPTER 10

Continuing Your Career-Life Journey

"Life is a journey, not a destination."
— Ralph Waldo Emerson

This book, and the Career-Life Partnering Model, is designed to guide you in evaluating and prioritizing your career and life goals. Life and career are ongoing journeys, and taking time to reflect can help keep you aligned with what truly matters to you. The process requires effort, but by embracing the challenges and opportunities it reveals, you can move closer to a fulfilling career and life.

Remember, you are in control. You set the destination, map out your path, and take each step along the way. It is possible to create your own unique direction, challenge yourself, and achieve your desired outcomes in both your life and career.

Understanding Workforce Expectations

Managers understand that to build a sustainable organization, it is essential to understand and meet the evolving needs of the workforce. Retaining employees and fostering a strong workplace culture depends on developing an attractive employer/employee value proposition. It is also vital to recognize generational differences, especially among leaders and managers, as these influence communication styles, work preferences, and career expectations.

Managers and employees alike benefit from clear expectations and supportive environments that honor varied career and life values. By acknowledging these differences, organizations can foster greater collaboration and inclusivity.

Creating a Career-Life Vision (Aspiration)

Aligning your career goals with your life stage and values is key to ensuring the right conversations with mentors, managers, or partners. Having a clear vision for both your career and your personal life will help you prioritize what's most meaningful to you. Balancing career aspirations with life goals is challenging but achievable, and the Career-Life Partnering Model can help you navigate this path effectively.

Don't limit yourself by what you can see today. Push yourself to envision your career and life over the long term. Challenge yourself to create a career-life vision that excites you!

Owning Your Career-Life Path

The Career-Life Partnering Model, developed through practical mentoring, is grounded in a simple premise: You define and own your career and your life. The model evolved over time and from working with emerging professionals looking to shape their futures toward a "fulfilling career" or "happy life." I encourage you to find and focus on what resonates with you. Question your assumptions, cultivate a trusted group of advisors, and approach your path with an open mind and a clear vision.

Reflecting on Your Progress

Making time for regular career-life assessment is crucial. It offers you a chance to check whether you're on track or need to adjust your priorities. Life and career paths shift over time, so protect time to reflect on your achievements and determine what's next. Careers often demand flexibility to handle client needs, team expectations, or tight deadlines. I hope your career journey is both challenging and rewarding. But remember, your personal life deserves attention, too. Give as much to your personal goals as you do to your career aspirations.

A Lifelong Journey of Career-Life Partnering

Moving toward a healthy career-life partnership is a lifelong commitment. Even in the Transition phase of my own career, I continue to weigh career aspirations against life goals. Where should I focus my energy? Can I achieve everything I desire, or must I adjust my expectations? It's essential to ask these questions early in your career-life partnership journey so you can actively pursue what matters most before it's too late.

Besides your commitment, time is your greatest asset. How you choose to use it will likely determine your success and satisfaction in both career and life. You may not always see a direct path to fulfillment, but I assure you that sustained focus on your goals will bring success.

Planning Your Journey

Some people enjoy making detailed plans, while others prefer flexibility. My plans tend to be high-level, offering direction without rigid constraints. Find an approach that fits you—whether it's a checklist on your fridge or notes in your calendar. Invite support from mentors, friends, or family to craft a plan that's both inspiring and achievable. Set ambitious standards, pursue experiences that bring you joy, and shape your plan to serve your unique goals.

Summary

Congratulations, you are already on the right path to a successful career and a meaningful life! You have taken the time to learn how you can take both your career and your life into your own hands. There is likely nothing more important than a career-life partnership that you create, you own, and you celebrate.

A few last ideas for you to consider:

- ✓ **Understanding workforce expectations:** *Either as an employee or a manager, create an environment where you can develop a career-life partnership. You will benefit from the belief that a meaningful career and life can be constructed.*

- ✓ **Creating a career-life vision:** *Push yourself to see your long-term career and life goals. Look at the experiences, challenges, and opportunities you can create along your career-life journey.*

- ✓ **Owning your career and life path:** *Surround yourself with a team of supportive mentors, coaches, friends, and family. Believe in your plan and invest the time, energy, and money necessary to accomplish your goals.*

- ✓ **Reflecting on your progress:** *Take time to measure your progress. Be honest with your assessment and take actions to adjust your plan.*

- ✓ **A lifelong journey of career-life partnering:** *Your time and your commitment are your greatest gifts. You will have a long career-life journey. Stay true to your aspirations and goals.*

> ✓ ***Planning your journey:*** *Build a plan that works for you!*

In closing, my main purpose for writing this book and my previous book, **Own Your Career – No One Else Will,** was to give back to those who might need help seeing their way through the challenges of building a successful career and live a happy life. If you need any help in any way, please let me know. I can be contacted at **Paul.Goudreault@EnorinePartners.com** or visit my website at www.PaulGoudreault.com.

Your time and your commitment are your greatest gifts!

Afterword

The workplace is continuously changing, and you are in the middle, looking ahead and crafting your career. It is an exciting time to think about how we will work in the future. Current trends suggest that remote officing, virtual teams, and flexible assignments will continue to lead the way to a new workplace. Some of these changes will be challenged by employers seeking more traditional approaches to building the workforce.

The employment models of today will continue to change to attract and retain future employees. Today's career developers have many opportunities. In the past, companies could create an alliance with an employee by offering security and a range of benefits for the employee and their family. Gradually, companies have been changing their "psychological contracts" with their employees toward providing a job within the context of their short-term business objectives. Long-term employment security is a way of the past, and the employee can't rely on securing a job for a lifetime.

That makes career-life partnering even more important.

Acknowledgements

Thanking everyone who has helped me in my career would be impossible. Maybe one of my biggest lessons has been, "you cannot have a successful career without a lot of help along the way!"

I start with a big thank you to my mother, Jane DeMaso-Goudreault, a first-generation immigrant from Italy, who was passionate about education and gave me great self-esteem. She had a successful career herself, fighting all the odds in a "man's world." I also admire and thank my sister, Yvonne Caamal Canul, who demonstrated to me how a life passion can lead to a successful career. Thank you to my dad, Fernand Goudreault, who shared the spirit of travel and adventure.

Many coworkers have supported and "put up with me" over the years. I want to thank Carol Anne Heart, Bob Karls and Jerry Rick for believing in me and guiding my early career journey. Also, a thank you to my career colleagues Rosanna Ouellette, Gretchen Koehn, J.R. Toren, Raimond Baumans, Ann Massey, Joseph Sczurko, Les Panek, Bob Salazar, Bill MacDonald and Brian Ricketts. All of you have pushed me when I needed it and pulled me up to see the bigger picture.

Several personal mentors have helped me balance my career with my life. Many thanks to Steve Schroeder, Mike

Henley, Randi Yoder, Mike Enright, Russ Larimer, Olaf Pfannkuch, Herb Wright and Alex Linderman.

Appendix I

Career-Life Care Assessment

The purpose of this Career-Life Care Assessment is to provide general guidance on identifying the key areas of your career and life that are important to you. Both assessments have ten building blocks that you can use to assess your current career and life priorities. Each building blocks is described by an *ideal* position from which you can assess your opportunities and challenges. Your responses will help you build your Career-Life Partnering Plan and prioritize your critical actions.

Use the following rating scale to assess your current position against the ideal state.
Rating Scale:

1. **Not so much**
2. **In progress**
3. **Absolutely nailed it**

Career Building Block	Description	Rating	Notes
Career Aspiration	*Ideal:* I have developed a long-term career aspiration that guides my career decisions. I review my aspiration annually to be sure it remains aligned with both my professional and my life goals.		
Advisory Team	*Ideal:* I have assembled an advisory team that I can talk to about my career. My team includes internal and external mentors, career coaches, and a financial planner.		

Investing in Yourself	*Ideal:* I routinely look for opportunities to advance my professional and educational knowledge through research, course studies, certifications, and conferences.		
Career Plan	*Ideal:* I have a career plan that identifies my career opportunities over the next three to five years. My plan includes any gaps I need to fill to be positioned for my future roles. I review my career plan annually.		

Networking Matters	*Ideal:* I actively identify and connect with professional relationships outside my advisory team that can help me understand my industry and potentially provide me future opportunities.		
Organization	*Ideal:* I am aligned with my organization's culture and believe in its vision, mission, or purpose. I also believe that my organization will provide me with opportunities to achieve my career aspiration.		

Professional Brand	*Ideal:* I have developed a strong professional brand within my industry. My brand reflects positively on me and allows me to seek opportunities to advance my career.		
Effectiveness Matters	*Ideal:* I have a clear understanding of my accountabilities and I am very effective within my role. I often take on assignments beyond my role for the experience and exposure.		
Sitting in Front	*Ideal:* I keep updated on my organization's longer-term goals. I am proactive in promoting myself to leaders and decision makers within my organization.		

Making Your Mark	*Ideal:* I am contributing to the organization, our clients, my teams, and my colleagues. I bring a unique skill or perspective that helps our organization be more responsive and effective.		
TOTAL			

Scoring:

0-17 Informed: You are aware of the Career and Life Building Blocks that can help you achieve a career-life partnership. You may be new to your career or reinventing your career. You may have several actions you want to take to address your challenges. Start small, with the key challenges you feel will bring you the greatest value. Not all the career and life building blocks are created equal! Look for those opportunities and challenges in your career and life that you can take on now. You decide the importance of each building block and pursue your career-life partnership.

18–33 Enlightened: You have begun developing the necessary behaviors in support of achieving your career and life goals. Find ways to reinforce your behaviors to continue your development towards full career-life partnering. Your challenges and opportunities to enhance yourself will change over time; move forward with those that will help you over the next one to three years. You also have experience with what it takes to be successful, so leverage your success for additional progress. Prioritize and address those Career and Life Building Blocks you see appropriate.

34–50 Purposeful: You have achieved the behaviors to reach your career or life goals. Selectively address those Career and Life Building Blocks you see appropriate to sustain your desired outcomes. You have accomplished a lot; continue to project both your career and life forward. Challenge your career aspirations and life goals, convince yourself you are on the right track. Your action plan will likely be very specific on where you can help yourself the most. Your positive behaviors are in place. Reinforce your behaviors and address the remaining Career and Life Building Blocks you see helpful.

Let's now get a little more specific. Indicate your:

TOP 3 OPPORTUNITIES Career Building Blocks with a rating of 3

1.

2.

3.

TOP 3 CHALLENGES Career Building Blocks with a rating of 1

1.

2.

3.

Life Building Block	Description	Rating	Notes
Physical Well-Being	*Ideal:* I have developed a daily routine that protects time for me allows me to exercise, work out, or otherwise get the physical activity I need.		
Mental Well-Being	*Ideal:* I have developed routine activities that allow me to spend time reflecting on my emotional needs and I am engaged in positive activities that benefit my mental health.		
Friends	*Ideal:* I routinely engage with a close network of friends who support me and are a positive influence in my career and life. My friendships are diverse and very meaningful to me.		

Family	*Ideal:* I understand my role within my family, and I routinely support my family. I commit the time necessary to fulfill my familial responsibilities.		
Colleagues	*Ideal:* I actively identify and connect with work colleagues both in work and outside of work. I enjoy working with my colleagues and they are a strong reason I like my work.		
Spiritual	*Ideal:* I am actively involved in my spiritual development. I routinely find time to spend in meditation, at church, or pursuing other activities that keep me spiritually fulfilled.		
Community	*Ideal:* I participate in community volunteering or leadership roles that are aligned with my passions and that help those in need.		

Self-Care	*Ideal:* I routinely find ways to improve my life through active involvement in hobbies, reading, and connection with self. I regularly treat myself to activities that honor me.		
Continuous Learning	*Ideal:* I set annual goals for continuous learning and education, both within and outside my career requirements.		
Financial Flexibility	*Ideal:* I am on the right track to achieve my financial goals. I have a relationship with a financial advisor and routinely evaluate my wealth-creation goals.		
TOTAL			

Scoring:

0-17: Informed: You are aware of the Career and Life Building Blocks that can help you achieve a career-life partnership. You may be new to your career or reinventing your career. You may have several actions you want to take to address your challenges. Start small, with the key challenges you feel will bring you the greatest value. Not all the career and life building blocks are created equal! Look for those opportunities and challenges in your career and life that you can take on now. You decide the importance of each building block and pursue your career-life partnership.

18-33 Enlightened: You have begun developing the necessary behaviors in support of achieving your career and life goals. Find ways to reinforce your behaviors to continue your development towards full career-life partnering. Your challenges and opportunities to enhance yourself will change over time; move forward with those that will help you over the next one to three years. You also have experience with what it takes to be successful, so leverage your success for additional progress. Prioritize and address those Career and Life Building Blocks you see appropriate.

34–50 Purposeful: You have achieved the behaviors to reach your career or life goals. Selectively address those Career and Life Building Blocks you see appropriate to sustain your desired outcomes. You have accomplished a lot; continue to project both your career and life forward. Challenge your career aspirations and life goals, convince yourself you are on the right track. Your action plan will likely be very specific on where you can help yourself the most. Your positive behaviors are in place, reinforce your behaviors and address the remaining Career and Life Building Blocks you see helpful.

Let's now get a little more specific. Indicate your:

TOP 3 OPPORTUNITIES Life Building Blocks with a rating of 3

1.

2.

3.

TOP 3 CHALLENGES Life Building Blocks with a rating of 1

1.

2.

3.

Appendix II

Career-Life Partnering Matrix

Congratulations! You have completed your Career-Life Care Assessment and identified your opportunities and challenges in both your career and your life. As you know, your career and life needs will change over time; however, it is helpful to assess the path you are on frequently and make the necessary modifications along the way. Place yourself on your Career-Life Partnering Matrix:

LIFE PURPOSEFUL	WORK TO LIVE	PRIORITIZE YOUR CAREER	CAREER LIFE PARTNERING
LIFE ENLIGHTENED	LIFE OR CAREER	CONTINUE YOUR PARTNERING JOURNEY	PRIORITIZE YOUR LIFE
LIFE INFORMED	BEGIN YOUR PARTNERING JOURNEY	CAREER OR LIFE	LIVE TO WORK
	CAREER INFORMED	CAREER ENLIGHTENED	CAREER PURPOSEFUL

- **Beginning Your Partnering Journey:** As a new career develop, maybe in your Acquire or Develop career lifecycle stage, you could be just entering the workforce and developing a clear view on your career and life goals. This is absolutely OK! You have already started to identify the important building blocks in both your career and life. Give yourself time to explore career options and establish your life priorities.

- **Life or Career:** As you assess your current priorities, maybe you should consider asking yourself more questions about how you will achieve your career aspiration. Will you be pleased with the outcome of your career if you remain on the same path forward? You have identified your career building blocks that need attention. Put in the work to challenge your view of your career.

- **Career or Life:** Your current priorities are focused on developing your career. It may be time to reflect on your life goals and commit to enhancing your life building blocks. Will your current path allow you to achieve your life goals? Here is where you challenge yourself to give more effort in achieving your life goals.

- **Work to Live:** You may consider your commitments outside of your career more important than those within it. Maybe your career aspiration is taking a back seat to your pursuit of a healthy and happy life. You have chosen to put your life goals ahead of your career goals. Is your current path sustainable and will it provide you the freedom to continue your life's journey? Spending more time on your career building blocks could lead to a more satisfying career and life partnership.

- **Live to Work:** Working hard and setting your career goals ahead of your life goals maybe necessary at times. However, if you maintain a live-to-work mindset throughout your career journey, you are likely to miss out on a lot of life. Is your current path forward sustainable and will it allow you to reach your life goals? Spending more time on your life building blocks could lead to a more satisfying life and career partnership

- **Prioritize Your Career:** You have an opportunity to achieve a meaningful career-life partnership. You have developed the behaviors required to promote and advance your life and career goals. You have recognized the benefits of a healthy and happy life. Maintaining commitments to your life building blocks and further developing your career building blocks will move you to a career-life partnership.

- **Prioritize Your Life:** You have an opportunity to achieve a meaningful career-life partnership. You have developed the behaviors required to promote and advance your career and life goals. You have recognized the benefits of your career. Maintaining commitments to your career building blocks and further developing your life building blocks will move you to a career-life partnership.

- **Continue Your Partnering Journey:** You have been able to commit to both your career and your life priorities. You are addressing those important building blocks of both a successful career and a meaningful life. Continue your journey and keep those career and life goals ahead of you.

- **Career-Life Partnering:** Congratulations! You are in position to partner with you career and have the life you want and deserve. It is hard to develop the discipline to establish a career-life partnership and even harder to maintain the priorities and behaviors that got you to this relationship between your career and life. It was tough getting here, acknowledge that. Also know that it is even tougher staying here!

Appendix III

Career-Life Partnering Plan

The purpose of this Career-Life Partnering Plan is to provide you with a practical and simple approach to challenge yourself towards a meaningful career-life partnership. You have done the hard work necessary to understand where you are in your ADAPT Career Lifecycle and what opportunities and challenges remain in developing your Career-Life Building Blocks. Let's now take that information and map out the next three to five years for both career and life goals. You may need to fill some gaps or change your priorities, but it will be worth it.

Some considerations when developing your plan:

Set a destination you believe in. Your career and life aspirations should be aligned with your passion and unique to you. When your journey gets difficult, you will what to know your destination is worth the fight. This part of your plan might be the most difficult to create. It is easy to describe where you are today, it is much harder to project yourself into the future. Set aside some time to dream, to talk with you mentors, friends, and family. Remember, you don't need to be perfect. And sometimes you may think your aspirations are not achievable, but do not limit yourself!

Reach for the sky, but keep your feet planted on the ground. A favorite client of mine gave me this advice many years ago. Expect to accomplish big things but set tangible and achievable goals along the way. Achieving your goals is a great way to motivate you to do more. Inspect your goals and your ability to accomplish them regularly. Seek input from others, but don't let them measure your success. You will be the only one who really knows if you are on the right path to accomplishing your goals.

Celebrate your success. As you achieve your milestones along your career-life journey, be sure to celebrate your success with those who have helped you. One of the greatest joys you will have will be to recognize your accomplishments and share your success with other. Lastly, don't keep your plan quiet. Share it with your advisory team and your manager and include it in your professional/personal development plan with your organization.

STEP 1. Aspirations

Do you have a career aspiration? If yes, what is it?

> **Example:** I will have a career that is rewarding, builds relationships, and provides me financial comfort.

My career aspiration is:

STEP 2. ADAPT Lifecycle

What career lifecycle stage are you in now? What is your next career lifecycle stage? What do you need to do to prepare yourself for the next career lifecycle stage? Does your organization provide you the opportunity to move forward?

> **Example:** I am in the Acquire career lifecycle stage. My next stage is Develop. I need to prepare myself for a job, learn how to be in the workforce, and further refine my career aspirations.

My current career lifecycle stage is:

My next career lifecycle stage is:

What I need to do to prepare for my next career lifecycle stage:

STEP 3. Career and Life Building Blocks

What have you identified as your top three opportunities and challenges from your Career-Life Care Assessment? What specifically will you do to leverage your opportunities and address your challenges?

> **Example:** *Career Challenge - Advisory Team.* I will develop a relationship with both an internal and external mentor by the end of the year. *Life Opportunity - Family.* I will continue protect the time I spend with my family. We will make time this year for a family holiday.

	OPPORTUNITY	CHALLENGES
CAREER	- PROFESSIONAL BRAND - NETWORKING MATTERS -	- ADVISORY TEAM - CAREER ASPIRATION -
LIFE	- COMMUNITY - SPIRITUAL -	- WELL BEING - FINANCIAL FLEXIBILITY -

STEP 4. Three- and Five-Year Career Goals

What specific roles do you believe are best to move your career forward in three years? In five years? Are these roles available in your current organization?

> **Example:** *Three-Year Role - Senior Engineer.* I will seek a role that allows me to expand my technical background and execute larger projects. *Five-Year Role - Account Manager.* I will become an account manager in five years. I will leverage my technical skills to build business relationships with key clients.

My three-year role target is:

Where is this role available in the organization?

My five-year role target is:

Where is this role available in the organization?

STEP 5. Three- and Five-Year Life Goals

What are the specific goals you believe are consistent with you desired life? What cn you do to explore your passion and build your relationships outside of work in three years? In five years?+

> **Example:** *Three-Year Goals:* Buy a house/condo and pay off my student loans. *Five-Year Goals:* Relocate closer to family, take a long adventure, and have $100,000 in my retirement account.

My three-year life goals are:

My five-year life goals are:

STEP 6. Career and Life Gaps

What actions/gaps do you need to take to achieve your role and goal expectations? What personal or professional improvements do you need to make to achieve your longer-term goals in three years? In five years?

> **Example:** *Three-Year Career Goal:* Get my Professional Registration. *Five-Year Career Goal:* Get my MBA and get a new client. *Three-Year Life Goal:* Save for my house down payment. *Five-Year Life Goal:* Maximize my retirement contributions.

STEP 7. Career-Life Roadmap

Let's put your plan on a map. Continue on your career-life partner journey!

Example: Career-Life Roadmap.

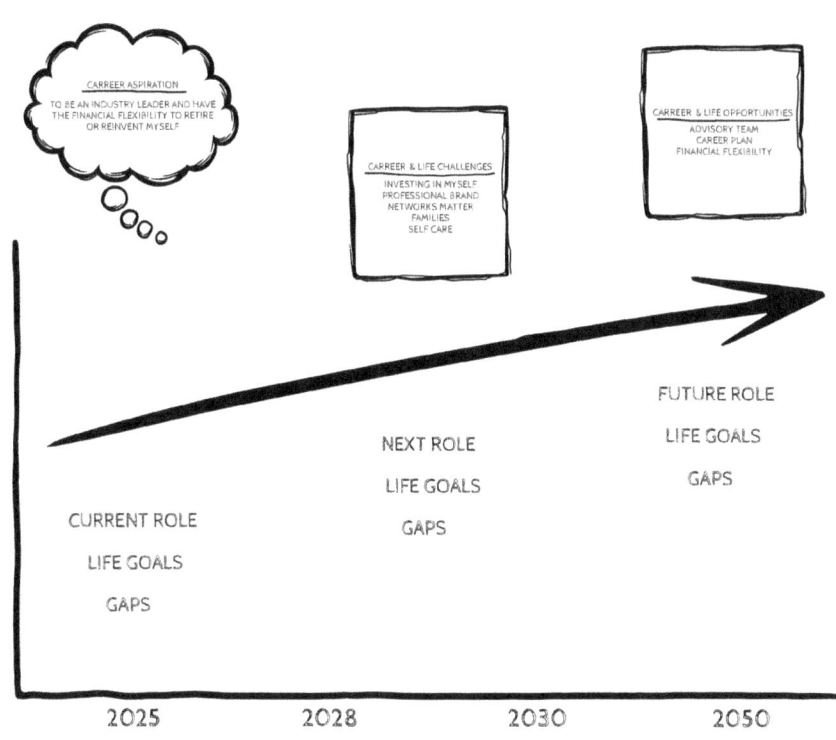

ABOUT THE AUTHOR

Paul Goudreault is an executive leader with over forty years of experience. He has served as CEO of two multinational environmental consulting firms and CEO of a manufacturing company. As the Founding Partner of Enorine Partners, Paul mentors emerging leaders and advances employee career growth.
Paul has built a global career in engineering and consulting, working in thirty countries and leading $2 billion in sales. Passionate about environmental stewardship, he has served on multiple nonprofit boards. Paul has been happily married for forty-five years to his wife, Katie, with two children, Monet and Adrien.
Stay connected at www.EnorinePartners.com or
Paul.Goudreault@EnorinePartners.com.

www.ingramcontent.com/pod-product-compliance
Lightning Source LLC
Chambersburg PA
CBHW071239070526
44583CB00017B/2251